W9-DBC-482

Theory and Practice

A Primer for Students of Applied Ethics

2nd Edition

L. M. Bernhardt

1st Edition Copyright © 2014 Laura M. Bernhardt

2nd Edition: 2017

Cover photo copyright © 2017 Laura M. Bernhardt

All rights reserved

ISBN: 1542532205

ISBN-13: 978-1542532204

DEDICATION

Dedicated, again, to my family (dogs, scholars, and musicians included).

CONTENTS

PREFACE

There are many excellent books in the field of applied ethics on the market today -- so many, in fact, that it is hard to imagine that anyone could want another. Why should I write and publish a book of my own, instead of simply using one of the many texts currently available for undergraduates?

The answer is simple: As good as those books are, they do not do certain things in precisely the way I want those things done.

When I first started teaching professional ethics online in addition to my face-to-face classes, I noticed that my online students were having an especially difficult time understanding the various ethical approaches (consequentialism, deontological ethics, etc.) that they were supposed to be learning to apply to issues in the professions. Their comprehension issues seemed to be the result of a combination of difficult material and too little time. While the assigned textbook was written in a style meant to be accessible to students with no prior experience in philosophy, it did what many readers in applied ethics do -- it offered a nice, comprehensive overview chapter on the major theoretical perspectives and then turned the students loose on scholarly articles more specific to ethics in the professions. The class had very little time to understand enough theory to do good philosophical work on those articles. It was, I discovered, nearly impossible for them to perform this task well, no matter how diligent they were.

My online students also did not really seem to understand what it meant to *apply* a theoretical perspective to a situation or problem. Instead of *making* an argument, they would often confine themselves to *mentioning* it: "It just seems to me that this is related to virtue ethics, because it affects my character and values." Because most of my online students had no background in philosophy (the course had no prerequisites), they simply hadn't received any training in the practices typical of the discipline. This meant that the students didn't get as much out of the rest of the articles in the assigned text as they could have – through no fault of their own, they didn't have the tools to evaluate and respond to the arguments being made.

In order to address these problems, I decided to redesign the online course. I built the new version around case study work, and my revised design required whole weeks spent on individual normative approaches. I decided that I would develop some brief lectures on a set of normative ethical theories and provide further instructional examples to illustrate how to put those theories into practice. Those lectures grew in the writing, and eventually became a book. In the second edition, I've made a few organizational changes and added material (cases and questions) in response to comments from users, but otherwise the text remains largely the same.

ACKNOWLEDGEMENTS

This book would not exist without the encouragement and support of my friends, colleagues, and students at Buena Vista University. Thank you all! I am also grateful for the very helpful feedback I received from faculty using the book at Lamar University in Beaumont, TX, some of whose excellent suggestions I have tried to include in the second edition.

INTRODUCTION

It is traditional to begin introductory chapters in books of this sort with a question: What is *ethics*? The text that follows may then lay out a set of definitions and approaches that purport to answer that question, thus preparing a foundation for the work to come. I would like, however, to begin with a slightly different question, the one that lies at the heart of so many of our ethical concerns: *What ought I to do?*

Obviously, there are different contexts in which such a question might be asked. If I am lost in my travels and come to an unfamiliar intersection, I can ask someone what I ought to do. In that case, it seems clear that what I'm asking is not really an *ethical* question -- I'm simply asking which way I ought to turn in order to reach my destination. If, on the other hand, I am confused about whether or not I should lie in order to spare a friend's feelings, my question seems to be of a different sort. Its answer becomes a matter of determining what constitutes good behavior as such. I am trying, when I ask what I ought to do in that situation, to determine whether or not *lying itself* is good or bad in a sense that implies a particular kind of value attaching to the choice. The word that is conventionally used to represent that kind of value is *morality*. Asking for street directions isn't usually a moral issue, but asking about whether or not to deceive someone invariably is. Think of the study of ethics, then, as a study of moral value (as distinct from things like monetary value, for example).

There are many different ways to engage in the study of ethics. One may, for example, choose to work on figuring out the nature of moral value; is there any absolute good, or is all "good" measured relative to some arbitrary social or personal standard? One might also spend one's time observing how various societies and individuals make and justify moral decisions. The kind of ethical study in this book, however, is the study of what philosophers call *normative* ethics; that's what we're doing when we try to find answers to the question of what one ought to do, morally speaking, and come up with good justifications for those answers.

This book isn't just about normative ethics, though. It's also about *applied* or *practical* ethics. When we study normative ethics, we're usually trying to find a system or method for making and evaluating moral judgments. When we study applied ethics, we're often trying to find solutions to specific moral problems. At the most elementary level, the difference between them amounts to the difference between asking what one ought to do *as a rule* and asking what one ought to do *in this case* (or, to be a bit more precise, in cases of this kind). Applied ethics may also include discussions about motives for action and principles for specific kinds of situations or contexts. So, in order to do applied ethics, it appears that we need at least two things: normative ethical theories and problems to which to apply them. The job of this book is to provide examples of normative ethical theory, which readers may then apply to cases of their own, and some models for applying theories to problems.

To that end, I have selected four kinds of normative ethical theory: virtue ethics, deontological ethics, utilitarianism/consequentialism, and the ethics of care. These four examples of normative theory are not all of the possible options one might have, but they represent typical approaches in the field. I've limited the number of theoretical perspectives here in order to keep the task of learning how to apply them manageable for an undergraduate audience with little or no background in philosophy and relatively little time to become competent where theory is concerned. I have also narrowed the field quite a bit in each theoretical area. While it is common to include both Kant and Ross in a solid, basic account of deontological ethics, I have confined myself to Kant. It seems to me that getting Kant right is quite difficult enough without throwing Ross into the mix. I have spent more time with the classical utilitarians (Bentham and Mill) than with contemporary forms of consequentialism, primarily because I have found that students do better with the latter when they've had the chance to become acquainted with the former. The chapter on the ethics of care represents an attempt to come up with a reasonable amalgam that includes a wide range of different approaches to the subject.

Each of the first four chapters in this book is devoted to a single kind of normative ethical theory, and they are all organized in the same way. I begin with a very brief historical note and then describe the theory itself. My descriptions of the various theories are necessarily simplified. There are nuances that I have deliberately ignored in some cases, usually because my aim is to generate a workable account for the purpose of application. One simply cannot boil the entirety of Kant's work on practical reason or all of the many different consequentialist arguments down to a few pages without making a few cuts, for example. I have also, for the most part, confined myself to fairly basic accounts of famous versions of the theories in question, looking mostly to the history of philosophy rather than to more current research. My intent is to provide a foundation for beginners, and I find the historical examples more helpful for realizing that intent than contemporary arguments, which tend to be more useful for people with a deeper acquaintance with the literature.

Once an applicable version of the theory is done, I turn to an example of how to use it. I use the same moral problem in all of the four theory chapters; I find that applying several approaches to a single case helps to clarify the similarities and differences among normative theories. This sample application case also makes it possible for me to discuss typical critical responses to each theory, so that students may see a model of how to raise and address objections. I have tried to limit myself to objections that address the usefulness of each theory for solving the problems they are supposed to solve, rather than criticisms aimed at the grounds for the theory itself; for the purpose of application, that seems to me to be the most useful approach to objections. There is a brief list of sources cited at the end of each chapter, so that students may (if they choose) go to the original sources in order to develop a better understanding of the material.

Once the theoretical foundations are laid, I offer an extended case study, so that students who want to see how to apply normative theories to complex real-life problems can have some idea how it is done. My goal is to model both how to write up a case and how make an argument about that case, using two of the theories given in this text in order to provide fuel for the ethical fire.

The remaining chapters feature short cases and discussion questions for each case. These chapters function as a sort of workbook, providing students with the opportunity to use the questions for guidance in forming their own arguments in response to the cases described. I've drawn the cases for these chapters from different subfields of applied ethics, so that there's a reasonably broad range of puzzles and issues to discuss.

The rest of this introductory chapter is devoted to work on some basic skills for doing the work at hand: modeling the application of theories to problems and a presenting a short guide to creating and responding to arguments.

I do not pretend for a moment that this text is exhaustive, authoritative, or complete. My hope, however, is that it will at least be useful.

Moving From Theory to Practice: A Brief Demonstration

What does it really mean to apply a theory to a moral problem? Merely matching a situation up against a theory is not the same thing as *applying* it. The whole point of applying a theory in the context of a discussion of ethical decision-making is that one is using it as a method for reasoning about moral problems. The theory provides a framework for the decision-making process -- it helps us to ask and to answer questions about what we ought to do and why.

Imagine, for example, that you are walking down the street and you see someone's wallet fall out of her bag. You are the only person who sees this happen -- indeed, you and she are the only other people walking down that particular street at that moment. You have to decide what to do. Should you call out to the person who dropped it? Should you chase after her? Is it even possible for you to do either of those things? If it isn't, should you keep the wallet? Should you give it to the police? Should you take it home, and perhaps use the personal information the wallet might contain in order to contact its owner and arrange for its return? Should you leave it where it is on the sidewalk, hoping that she might realize she's lost it and come back?

Your first step is to evaluate the various choices in order to determine which one is correct. But how? Let's say that you commit yourself to the proposition that what makes a choice or an act good lies in the consequences that follow from it. If it's more likely to have a "good" result, then you should do it. Of course, that leaves you with a question: how do you decide what would count as a "good" result? Perhaps in this case, you decide that a good result is the one that causes the least harm, and that a bad result is the one that causes the most harm. You will naturally have to come up with some reasonable idea of what "harm" is. You will probably also want to make sure to decide whose harm is relevant to your calculations; obviously you and the owner of the wallet are relevant parties, but is there anyone else who might matter? *All of these decisions and commitments and questions are the business of normative ethical theory.*

While you deliberate, the wallet's owner moves on down the street, and you can no longer see where she's gone. That eliminates some of your options (chasing after her, shouting after her to get her attention). Now: in order to cause the least harm to the relevant participants (you limit this to yourself and the wallet's owner), what should you do? Keeping the wallet seems to you to be out of the question -- while it might benefit you to keep it, the loss of her identification, her cash, her credit cards, and any other items of importance or value in the wallet would definitely do some harm to the wallet's owner. You don't think that leaving the wallet on the sidewalk is a great option either -- harm to the wallet's owner caused by its loss is highly likely to occur whether you steal it or leave it behind. That seems to leave you with at least two options related to picking the wallet up: do you turn the wallet over to the police, or do you go through the wallet yourself in order to contact its owner and return it (either in person or in some other way, perhaps by mail)? Your decision, no matter what you choose, will be made with your theoretical rule in mind: which option yields the least harmful result?

This is what applying an ethical theory to a situation looks like. In the case I've just described, the theory in use is a simple sort of consequentialism. Applying it means using it to guide the process of figuring out the right thing to do.

Applying theory in this way makes it possible to argue in support of the correctness of one's choices. The broad outline of such an argument looks something like this: If it's true that what makes a choice morally good is whether or not it yields good consequences, and if it's true that what makes consequences good is that they cause the least possible amount of harm, and if [choice x] is the option most likely to yield the least harmful consequences, then [choice x] is a morally good choice to make.

Obviously this argument isn't perfect – a number of its components require further work if they are to be at all convincing to a critical audience. It is, however, a fair model of the kind of thing that happens when one does applied or practical ethics. It is a good start. It is where *you* should start, once you've had the chance to study the normative ethical theories described in this book!

Making an Argument by Using a Theory

In the previous section, you saw a broad outline for an argument in favor of some decision or other relative to the case of the dropped wallet. That outline consisted of a set of conditional (if-then) statements in support of whatever choice you happened to make. Let's list those statements in a slightly different way in order to get a clearer picture of how an argument of this sort works:

If all of the following are true:

1. The moral goodness of a choice depends on whether or not it yields good consequences
2. What makes any given set of consequences good is that they cause the least possible amount of harm
3. Choice *x* (whatever that might be) is the option that yields the least harmful consequences

Then it must be true that:

4. Choice *x*'s consequences are good, therefore
5. Choice *x* is a morally good choice.

We'll call numbers 1-3 the *premises* of our argument, number 4 is an *intermediate conclusion* and number 5 is the *conclusion* of the entire argument. Premises and conclusions are the basic pieces of which arguments are made, and the general idea when you build an argument is to assemble a set of premises (reasons, really) that, if true, logically imply the truth of the conclusion. Notice that premise 1 and premise 2 represent the claims of a normative ethical theory (a form of consequentialism, as mentioned above). The argument proceeds from taking those claims to be true to premise 3 and intermediate conclusion 4, which relate the case at hand to the theoretical claims in 1 and 2 by stating that [choice *x*] represents an example of what's asserted in the theory. The intermediate conclusion in 4 extends the logical implications of the theoretical claims and the example to which they apply to draw the final conclusion in 5. This is what it looks like when we apply a normative theory to a situation or case – we lay out what the theory claims, present the case in the context of those claims, and draw our conclusion from the conjunction of theoretical claims and case features.

Raising and Responding to Objections

Now that we've laid our argument out a bit more clearly, let's start thinking about how to respond critically to what it claims. The entire thing is conditional, after all: *if* the premises are true, *then* the conclusion is true. But what happens if someone doesn't agree that all of these things are true? It's entirely possible that the audience for any argument might come up with an *objection* – that is, someone might poke holes in the premises or otherwise undermine the reasoning being used and thereby make the argument weaker and less convincing.

Coming up with good objections is an important part of dealing both with the arguments other people make and with the arguments we make ourselves. In addition to using objections to respond critically to other people's arguments, we also ought to raise and answer objections as a part of making *our own* arguments stronger. Don't be afraid to look for the flaws in your case and find ways to repair them. This also allows you to preemptively defend your argument against criticism.

If you are unsure of how to come up with a good objection, consider the following suggestions:

1) Good objections tend to address the *premises* of an argument. That is, they are aimed at the reasons given in support of the argument's conclusion rather than the conclusion itself. Are the facts described in the premises correct? Are there pieces missing from a definition given in a premise, or exceptions to some rule used there?

2) An objection may either introduce new information or reconsider the correctness of present information.

3) An objection is also an argument, and requires the same amount of careful thought and logical support as the original argument to which it responds.

4) It is possible to agree with an argument's conclusion but not with the reasoning offered in support of that conclusion. It is often worthwhile to reject a given set of premises and then suggest a better way to make the same point.

A Short Note On Method

One of the central goals of this book is to offer students the opportunity to practice the application of normative ethical principles to ethical problems. The text assumes that students will be looking at case studies or dilemmas written for the purpose of studying and testing those normative principles in order to develop good arguments in support of their own conclusions. Consider using these four steps as a basic procedure for doing these things.

Step 1: Identify the Relevant Features of the Problem

While the full description of the problem in any given case itself contains a wealth of potentially important information, not every detail in the story is morally relevant. In the example of the lost wallet, it probably doesn't matter what the weather is, or what color the wallet is, or what the wallet is made of. The kinds of harm that might be caused to the wallet's owner by losing the wallet, however, are important.

Step 2: Identify the Applicable Elements of the Theory

Not all of the features of a given normative theory are relevant for the purpose of application. Some ethical theories cover rather a lot of ground, including concerns about human life in general, assumptions about the nature of rationality, etc. Some of those things may be helpful, but some may not. Think carefully about what exactly you want to argue as you try to decide which bits of the theory you need in order to make your argument and which bits can be assumed or omitted.

Step 3: Use Those Elements to Address the Problem

Completing steps one and two should reveal a clear set of core issues and the theoretical tools needed to address those issues. The next thing to do is to see what those theoretical tools do when used on the issues at hand.

Step 4: Consider Objections

Very rarely is a solution perfect. One way to test how well a chosen solution works is to imagine and to address possible failings, using the method described on the previous page.

PART 1:

EXPLORING NORMATIVE THEORIES

Theory and Practice

VIRTUE ETHICS

The origins of what we call *virtue ethics* in the Western tradition lie in ancient Greece, particularly in the philosophical work of Aristotle (384-322 BCE).[1] In his *Nicomachean Ethics,* Aristotle offers a set of claims about what constitutes the best sort of human life, and he does so by articulating a theory in which acquiring the best sort of human life depends to a significant degree on the cultivation of *virtue.*

Before I go on, it's important at this point to pay special attention to the wording of that last sentence. Aristotle's argument in *Nicomachean Ethics* isn't about how to make or evaluate individual moral choices. It's about what sort of person one ought to become, and what sort of life one ought to live. In other words, virtue ethics of the Aristotelian kind is really about establishing the conditions of character under which good choices might be made rather than supplying a method for choosing. For practical purposes, this means that it is probably most useful to think of the work of applying this form of ethical theory to cases in terms of how well our choices serve the overall goal or end of supporting the best sort of human life, which we'll call the *highest good.*

Aristotelian virtue ethics begins by characterizing the highest good toward which all human activity is aimed as something called *eudaimonia.* While this term is often translated as "happiness," it is probably more accurate to understand *eudaimonia* as "well-being" or "flourishing."[2] More specifically, Aristotle says that *eudaimonia* is "activity of the soul in accord with virtue" over the course of a "complete life," rather than a feeling.[3] The word "virtue" in this context is one way to translate the Greek term *aretê,* which also may be rendered as "excellence" in English. For Aristotle, the virtue or excellence of a thing depends on its function – the virtue of a thing is the quality or set of qualities of that thing that enable it to fulfill its function well.[4] If the function of a knife is to cut, for example, then the virtue of a knife lies in its sharpness (the quality of the knife that, when present, makes it cut well).

What is the function of a human being? Human beings are obviously quite a bit more complicated than cutlery. According to Aristotle, the function (and therefore the virtue) of human beings is to be found in the feature that distinguishes them from other forms of life: *rationality*.[5] The best sort of life for such a being is a life of reason, characterized by contemplation and self-awareness. To be virtuous, if our function as human beings is determined by our rational nature, is to possess, exercise, and maintain the qualities that support that reasoned and reasonable life.

The tricky bit, however, is figuring out what exactly those qualities are. Aristotelian virtue consists of a *mean* between two extremes (vices) – one of excess and one of deficiency. Bravery, for example, is the virtue concerned with the appropriate response to frightening things. It is the mean between the vices of rashness (excess) and cowardice (deficiency).[6] That mean is determined by reason (especially the form of reasoning called *phronesis*, which means practical wisdom or prudence), and it is measured against the features and situation of the individual making that determination. What is brave for a healthy and well-trained U.S. Marine, for example, might be rash for an elderly person with severe physical impairments and no military knowledge. While it might be cowardly for that Marine to retreat in fear from the typical combat situations for which Marines are uniquely prepared, it isn't at all cowardly for a small child to do so. Likewise, generosity is not measured in the same way for the rich and for the poor – it is measured in terms of what one has and how one might use or share one's resources appropriately.[7] There are even some forms of virtue – like magnificence, which is a kind of generosity exercised by those with very great wealth – that are really only available to certain people.[8] Just the same, it is entirely possible for anyone to be virtuous and to flourish as a human being, provided one puts in the right sort of work on oneself and finds the mean.

Virtues are acquired by a process of habituation that is also a process of self-examination and growth. One becomes brave, in effect, by doing brave things (relative to one's own determination of what the appropriate response to a frightful situation or condition is). One trains oneself to become virtuous by taking on virtuous behaviors as habits. What's more, one does not acquire virtues in isolation from each other – in order to attain *eudaimonia*, one has to acquire a full package of virtues (including things like bravery, temperance, generosity, etc.) under some notion of oneself that unites them into a rational whole.[9] It is not enough, for the purpose of attaining the best sort of human life, to be accidentally or occasionally virtuous. One must cultivate a whole life of the right sort, which means that the acquisition and maintenance of virtue is constant work.

It is also important to notice that virtue is not acquired in a vacuum –

for Aristotle, humans are fundamentally social beings, which means that virtue itself is acquired and exercised in the company of others.[10] It is not an accident that he spends quite a lot of time and effort talking about friendship in the middle of a discussion of virtue – it is "necessary for our life," and "no one would choose to live without friends even if he had all other goods."[11] It is in our relationships with others that we are able to acquire and refine virtuous habits, which is one of the main reasons why friendship is also "fine" and praiseworthy.[12]

For applied ethics, this kind of view presents at least one obvious difficulty: there appear to be no clear *rules* for virtuous choosing that a person might use to frame the decision-making process. There is also no tidy, fixed list of the virtues themselves. Later thinkers have, over the years, come up with their own accounts of virtue and their own lists of virtues; some religious traditions, for example, have their own notions about what virtue is and which behaviors count as virtuous. Even without listing rules and virtues, it is nonetheless possible to use a virtue-ethical approach to address specific problems, both for individuals and for groups. What is required is a process of practical reasoning in which one attempts to find the mean, always keeping in mind the ultimate goal of supporting human flourishing or well-being.[13]

In this chapter and the three that follow, I use a single sample dilemma in which a moral decision must be made. Ideally, because I am applying each of the normative theories discussed in this book to the same situation, it should be a little easier to see how these theories are related to each other and how they may be used in response to each other. The point of these examples is not necessarily to provide ideal or authoritative solutions to the sample dilemma. My aim is a more modest one: to demonstrate some of the reasoning processes suggested by the normative approaches under consideration. As a part of each demonstration, I will also address a few possible objections in order to stimulate further thinking about the arguments.

Infidelity and The Demands of Friendship

Imagine that you have two friends, Kelly and Taylor (imagine them to have whatever combination of gender identities suits your fancy). You have known them both for a very long time, and you are equally close to both of them. They have been in a long-term, committed relationship with each other for nearly 15 years, and you have always thought of their relationship as an especially happy and well-adjusted one. They have two children together – a pre-teen and a toddler. They own a home together, and they both share the burden of child rearing and working outside the home. They seem to you to have an ideal life together, and they seem very happy.

One evening, as you are entering a bar with some of your coworkers to enjoy a little happy hour cheer, you notice that Kelly is sitting in a corner booth with someone. At first, you think that this person is Taylor, but you can't see clearly around the high sides of the booth. Just as you are about to wave to Kelly and perhaps go over to say hello, your cell phone rings. The caller is Taylor, who wants to chat briefly about a neighborhood watch meeting you both plan to attend tomorrow. In the course of your short conversation, it becomes clear to you that Taylor believes that Kelly is still in a meeting at work. This makes you uncomfortable, but for the moment you shrug it off and don't say anything; it's entirely possible that Kelly's at the bar with someone from work, and that they are having their meeting there. Because you don't want to interrupt, you stand your coworkers to a round of drinks and don't greet Kelly.

Later in the week, you see Kelly again in an unexpected place, this time seated a few rows ahead of you at the movies. Kelly is with a stranger, and they are behaving as if they are intimate with each other. They appear to be on a date. This makes you more than uncomfortable – you find it profoundly disturbing. You are unwilling to cause a public scene, so you don't confront Kelly there. Instead, you arrange to have lunch with Kelly alone a few days later in order to discuss things.

Over lunch, you tell Kelly what you've seen and ask for an explanation. Kelly reluctantly confesses that things have not being going well at home – Taylor has been busy with work and childcare and other activities, and doesn't seem to have time to give Kelly the kind of attention that used to characterize their relationship. Kelly, feeling lonely, has pursued a sexual relationship with a married coworker who is in similar straits. Neither participant in the affair sees it as anything serious, emotionally speaking – they are simply "friends with benefits," two lonely people whose primary relationships are not answering their needs where sexual intimacy is concerned. Kelly does not believe that this arrangement is a real threat to Kelly's commitment to Taylor, and intends to break off the affair eventually. Both parties to the affair are practicing safe sex, and they are making every effort to be discreet. You are the only person so far to catch them, as far as they know; their respective partners are entirely ignorant of the affair.

Kelly asks you, as a friend, to keep the affair secret, and promises to break it off as soon as possible and then tell Taylor all about it. You are torn. Kelly and Taylor are both very important to you, and you don't want to risk your friendship with either of them. What should you do? Should you keep Kelly's secret (trusting Kelly to break off the affair and repair things with Taylor), or should you tell Taylor what you now know about Kelly's infidelity?

Following the Path of Virtue

How should a virtue ethicist respond to a problem like this? To begin with, it is necessary to identify the central elements of the problem. One clear difficulty lies in the conflicting demands placed upon your friendship by Kelly and Taylor. Keeping Kelly's secret is certainly something that serves your relationship with Kelly, but it betrays your relationship with Taylor. Conversely, telling Taylor about what you've discovered betrays Kelly's confidence in service to your relationship with Taylor. More generally speaking, you are being asked to engage in an act of deceit.

Figuring out what constitutes the best human life as such doesn't really seem helpful in this situation. The narrower question of what you can do to promote virtue in your own life and in the lives of your friends, however, is exactly the thing to ask in order to find an appropriate way to deal with this dilemma. If you can find the mean, you can make decisions that are more likely to promote well-being in yourself and in others, and thereby contribute to the creation of best sort of life.

The matter of whether or not one ought to engage in deceit lends itself pretty easily to analysis in terms of virtue. Think of truthfulness as the mean between an excess – rudeness, perhaps – and a deficiency (deceitfulness).[14] Kelly is definitely *not* being virtuous in deceiving Taylor, and asking you to do the same is not an act that promotes virtue in you; dishonesty, even for a friend's sake, remains dishonest. Your own truthfulness, however, is not the only issue at hand. You must also consider your relationships with Kelly and Taylor. If they are truly your friends, then you should want what is best *for* them and what is best *from* them; as much as you desire *eudaimonia* for yourself, if they are truly your friends, you should also desire it for them. It obviously isn't possible for you to choose virtuously *for* someone else, but it *is* possible for you to make choices that are more likely than not to promote virtue both in yourself and in others. Choosing to lie or to otherwise conceal the truth from Taylor at Kelly's behest is out of the question on those terms. If truthfulness is virtuous for you, it is also virtuous for Kelly, and you cannot promote Kelly's flourishing by enabling Kelly's vices.

That said, remember that for an Aristotelian virtue ethicist, truthfulness is as much about revealing the truth *appropriately* as it is about being honest. If you are to reveal the truth to Taylor, you must not only be truthful, but also mindful of the way in which you tell that truth. Honesty is not quite the same as truthfulness in this context; running immediately off to tell Taylor about the affair is honest, but it might not be the most appropriate way to be truthful. Shouting the news at Taylor across a crowded store, for example, would be honest but also entirely inappropriate. Finding a time and place to meet privately with Taylor would plainly be a better way to handle things. Furthermore, while simply laying out the whole sordid business for Taylor might be the truthful thing to do, and while it might also be the best way to promote not only your own virtue but Kelly's, it may still be unnecessarily hurtful to Taylor. It could also prove harmful to the already troubled relationship between Kelly and Taylor; they might be able to work things out in a less hurtful way without your interference than they would if you are the one to reveal Kelly's indiscretion to Taylor. If their relationship really is important to their mutual and their respective individual well-being, and if their flourishing is also important to you, then it should probably be your priority to see to it that you do not undermine the possibility that they might repair things. Your truthfulness, in order to be properly virtuous, must include taking all of these things seriously.

What should you do? You cannot be absolutely certain that Kelly will keep the promise to end the affair and confess it to Taylor; after all, Kelly has already demonstrated a propensity for deceit. You need to find a solution that promotes appropriate truthfulness for all parties and respects the relationships involved. The solution that seems best to you in light of all of these considerations begins with an ultimatum: You tell Kelly that in one week, if you have not heard from both Kelly and Taylor that they've had a truthful discussion about the affair, you will go to Taylor yourself and reveal everything you know about it. This seems to you to be the only way to manage all of the concerns involved – it commits you and Kelly to truthfulness and puts some pressure on Kelly to follow through with the promise to end the affair.

Kelly does not think much of your solution, and suggests that revealing the truth to Taylor may in fact do more harm than good. It could damage the relationship beyond repair, while ending the affair and keeping it completely secret would allow the relationship to continue and allow some time for Kelly to work on finding ways to address the problems between them. If that relationship is important to their flourishing, it would be wrong (Kelly suggests) to damage it in this way. You could also be damaging a further set of relationships: those between Kelly and Taylor and their children. That damage could present a serious obstacle to the children's well-being.

You are understandably skeptical of Kelly's concern about damaging the relationship, given the fact that the only reason the affair hasn't already ruined things completely is because Taylor doesn't know about it yet. You point out that if the relationship between them cannot be repaired, that may ultimately be a good outcome for them both, albeit not without difficulty in the near term. Your aim is to promote your own flourishing, Kelly's flourishing, and Taylor's flourishing, which requires promoting their virtue as well has their comfort and happiness. A relationship in which a deceit remains buried is not one conducive to promoting that goal, regardless of whether it is your friendship with this couple or their committed relationship to each other. Kelly's worry about the flourishing of their children looks a bit more serious, but it does not convince you to change your mind. If Kelly and Taylor want their children to flourish (and therefore want to promote the development of virtue), that cannot be done in a context in which they do not work toward their own virtue as well.

Kelly's final moment of resistance comes in the form of a threat to reject your friendship if you go through with your plan. You remind Kelly that while that would be a sad thing, a friendship in which virtue is already impaired by deceit would cease to serve as a boon to flourishing for either party. You stand by your original plan.

NOTES

---

[1] There are also healthy strains of virtue-ethical theory in non-Western traditions, particularly in the work of the Chinese Confucians. In this chapter, I am limiting the scope of my discussion to Aristotelian ethics as representative of the basic form virtue ethics takes in the Greek tradition.

[2] Terence Irwin, "Glossary: Happiness," in Aristotle, *Nicomachean Ethics*, 2nd ed., Terence Irwin trans. (Indianapolis: Hackett Publishing Company Inc., 1999), 333.

[3] Aristotle, *Nicomachean Ethics*, 2nd ed., Terence Irwin trans. (Indianapolis: Hackett Publishing Company Inc., 1999), 1098a17-19. [hereafter NE]

[4] This is the implication of the discussion of function and virtue in NE between 1097b25 and 1098a20.

[5] NE 1098a1-20.

[6] NE 1115a10-1117a20.

[7] NE 1119b25-1122a17.

[8] NE 1122a20-1123a20.

[9] See especially the discussion of magnanimity as crowning virtue (NE 1123a35-1125a35) and relate it to the life of *theoria* or study (NE 1177a15-1197a30).

[10] See, for example, the discussion of the human good as social at NE 1097b9.

[11] NE 1155a5-6. "Friendship" in this context apparently refers to many different kinds of social relations, including those between parents, acquaintances, etc.

[12] NE 1155a30.

[13] NE 1109b7-11. In the passage that runs from 1109a20 to 1109b25, Aristotle lays out a program for reaching the mean in general that strongly suggests the importance of temperance, prudence, and deep and constant self-examination for attaining virtue and building the best sort of human life.

[14] I'm using a slightly different sense of "truthfulness" here than Aristotle does – Aristotle's discussion of "truthfulness" is about not boasting about one's qualities or being excessively self-deprecating. See NE 1127a15-1127b30.

DEONTOLOGICAL ETHICS

The main concern of deontological ethics is with *obligation*, and deontological theories are frequently outlined in terms of identifying, classifying, and justifying *duties*. Perhaps the most important philosophical proponent of this view is Immanuel Kant (1724-1804). Kant's moral theory is dauntingly complex. He works out its main features in at least three different books: the *Grounding for the Metaphysics of Morals,* the *Metaphysics of Morals* (including the *Doctrine of Right* and the *Doctrine of Virtue*), and the *Critique of Practical Reason.* While the most useful piece of his system for the purpose of practical application – The Categorical Imperative – can be stated relatively briefly, I'm going to begin by spending a little time laying out some of the foundational assumptions on which it depends before I explain what the Categorical Imperative is and how it works.

Kant begins the first part of the *Groundwork of the Metaphysics of Morals* with the assertion that "it is impossible to think of anything at all in the world, or indeed even beyond it, that could be considered good without limitation except a *good will.*"[1] Other qualities or talents may be good for some other purpose or reason, but the good will is good in itself, and is the thing that may make other qualities or talents good. A supremely clever serial killer, for example, gives the lie to the idea that being supremely clever is an unconditionally good quality, but cleverness can be good when it functions in conjunction with a good will. But what is it that makes the will good? At first glance, Kant's work looks a bit like the Aristotelian approach to character – having a good will seems rather a lot like having the best sort of ethical character. What makes Kant different?

In order to understand what Kant means by *good will,* the best place to begin is with an account of the will itself; note that in this context we are not talking about the feeling or quality of "good will," but are instead discussing what makes the human will (whatever that is) good. For Kant, the will is the power or faculty of choice – that is, the will is that feature of a rational being which chooses and generates action.[2] The will is motivated both by reason and by inclinations or urges. Sometimes, inclination is stronger, and one chooses in order to satisfy a desire, with reason working out how that is most effectively done. Sometimes, reason is stronger; in that case, reason drives the choice made, and inclination serves it. Typically, they interact with each other in a number of different ways in any given situation, and it isn't always clear which motivation is acting more powerfully on the will.

Consider the example from the introductory chapter of this book, in which a stranger drops her wallet on the street. In that situation, a person might experience any number of different desires or urges where the wallet is concerned – the desire to take the wallet and keep it, the desire to be helpful, the fear of being thought to be a thief, the desire for approval for returning it, hope for a reward, etc. If inclination is stronger than reason in determining the will, then reason is confined to figuring out how to satisfy some given desire. Reason, in the absence of the influence of inclination, merely asks whether or not it is right to take some given action (stealing the wallet, abandoning it, returning it). Sometimes, inclination and reason agree on a course of action – a choice is both desirable and right. Often they do not, and one is put in the position of choosing either to follow one's urges or to deny them.

Kant's firm conviction is that there is an important difference between a choice driven mainly by inclination and one driven mainly by reason, and it is the latter that may be said to have moral content. That means that even in cases in which urges and reason agree, the choice is only morally valuable if it is reason and not inclination that motivates the will to choose. **A truly good will is one determined by reason, not inclination.** This is what it means for Kant for the will to be motivated by *duty* – our duties or obligations are rationally determined as principles for action.[3] This doesn't mean that all rational choices are by definition good. One can quite rationally decide to do rather horrible things, which is typically the result of reason serving the inclinations instead of checking them (this is the rational behavior of a well-organized murderer, for example). Such choices do not count, ethically speaking, as good. In order for some given choice to count as having moral content, the final word on that choice lies with reason, not with inclinations made operational by reason.

How does reason arrive at duty? According to Kant, it does so by way of the *Categorical Imperative*. An imperative is an obligation or a command, and Kant identifies two types: hypothetical and categorical. Hypothetical imperatives – which do *not* give us our duties -- are always aimed toward some other end, and they all have the same conditional form: if I want to achieve goal x, I ought to take action y. If I want to build a house, for example, it is *hypothetically* imperative that I purchase tools and materials and make a plan. It is also hypothetically imperative that I take bids from contractors and arrange financing to pay them. Notice that a great many potentially contradictory things can be hypothetical imperatives, and the nature of the end has quite a lot to do with which means are hypothetically required in order to achieve that end. The things I hypothetically ought to do in order to build a brick house are not the same things I ought to do in order to build a straw house or a wooden one, for example. If my narrower end is to build not just a house, but a brick house, the things I ought to do are determined by that more specific end. A hypothetical imperative is always conditioned on the end I set, and these ends are typically chosen on the basis of some desire or inclination.

For an imperative to demand something categorically, however, is different. It means that the action required is an end in itself, and is not demanded for some other purpose. A hypothetical imperative is an if-then command; a categorical imperative, on the other hand, is absolute, and simply says "do *x*." If something is demanded of me categorically, then I ought to do it regardless of the situation or any other ends or desires I might have. Moral content or moral value occurs in choices driven by a categorical imperative, not a hypothetical imperative. This is how, according to Kant, we arrive at the moral law.

Kant asserts that there is really only one Categorical Imperative, expressible in at least three ways.[4] The first is often called the *Universal Law formulation*: "Act only in accordance with that maxim through which you can at the same time will that it become a universal law."[5] That is, only choose what you can at the same time will that everyone else ought to choose, as if it were a universal law. If you cannot will without contradiction that everyone ought to do it, then you should not do it – it is morally wrong. The classic example used to illustrate this formulation is *false promising*. If I ask you to loan me $100 and promise to pay you back on Tuesday, all the while having no intention whatsoever of paying you back, then I am violating the Categorical Imperative. Why? Because I cannot will that everyone's promises should be false and still expect my false promise to work. In a world in which all promises are false, you would never give me the money in the first place. In other words, I cannot will a universal law to which I am the only exception.

The second formulation of the Categorical Imperative is called the *Formula of Humanity*: "So act that you use humanity, whether in your own person or in the person of any other, always at the same time as an end, never merely as a means."[6] By this, Kant means that we are not to treat other people (rational beings) merely as things to be used to satisfy our own ends. Slavery, for example, is an obvious case in which a person is being used as a means to an end and not an end in him/herself. Paid employment, on the other hand, assuming it is done without deception or coercion, involves a contract between agents capable of making and committing to their own choices. If I offer to pay you to build a house for me, you are free to refuse, free to negotiate a price, etc. You are not, in that case, merely a tool for my use. False promising violates the Humanity Formulation because it is manipulative, undermining a person's freedom to choose – I deny you truthful information in order to make you give me the money, when you might otherwise refuse if you knew I wouldn't repay you.

The third form of the Categorical Imperative (which doesn't see as much use in applied ethics) is called *The Kingdom of Ends*, which essentially requires us to act as if we were both members and legislators of a moral community in which all other members/legislators come up with *and* comply with the moral law.[7] In effect, it is another rule against making oneself an exception. There is no room in the Kingdom for people who reason in favor of lying "because everyone else is doing it" – in the Kingdom, the basic presumption for all choosers is that *no one else is lying*. If false promising is wrong for any one reasoner in the Kingdom of Ends, it is wrong for all of them. In the Kingdom, one always treats all others as ends in themselves, and assumes that all others do likewise.

One tricky thing about applying the Categorical Imperative is figuring out exactly where it ought to be applied. There are any number of behaviors, for example, that seem irrelevant to the Categorical Imperative, or that hover in a sort of limbo because they are neither forbidden nor obviously required by duty. To address this problem, Kant introduces the distinction between *necessary* or *perfect* duties and *meritorious* or *imperfect* duties, where the former are absolutely required and the latter are vitally important for preserving the conditions under which attention to duty thrives. It is obligatory to preserve one's life (suicide is forbidden, because it negates the will completely); it is meritorious to cultivate one's skills and talents, in service to the further development of the power to choose effectively.[8]

There are also choices that seem to involve conflicts of duty. What happens, for example, when one is presented with the choice to lie (which fails the test of the Categorical Imperative) in order to save someone's life (which the Categorical Imperative may also demand)? The important point to remember in such cases is the distinction between hypothetical and categorical imperatives. It may certainly be *hypothetically* imperative to lie in order to save someone, but that will not make the lie morally good. The end does not justify the means for Kant. If a particular act is not morally correct considered as an end in itself, it will not become morally correct by being used as the means to a different, morally good end.

What Does Duty Demand?

How would you respond to Kelly's infidelity to Taylor if you were to think like a Kantian deontological ethicist? In order to discover the best moral decision to make, you have to apply the Categorical Imperative, and in order to apply the Categorical Imperative, you first have to identify the various ends in play.

Kelly is asking you to deceive Taylor in order to preserve your friendship and to protect Kelly's relationship with Taylor. Deception, considered as an end in itself, does not pass the test of the Categorical Imperative. Lies and other forms of deception only work to manipulate someone in a social world in which the expectation of truthfulness is the norm for human communication. If it were a universal law that everyone should always lie or deceive, then it would no longer be possible to manipulate others in this way. Deception also clearly requires using another person merely as a means to one's own end, without any real respect for that person's power to choose as a rational being. Deceiving Taylor, as Kelly has done and is now asking you to do, fails to meet the demands of the Categorical Imperative, and is therefore morally wrong. You tell Kelly you cannot deceive Taylor, and you cannot approve of Kelly's own deceit.

Kelly objects that what you are really being asked to do is not to lie to Taylor – you're being asked to preserve a set of friendships and other relationships (your friendship with Kelly, your friendship with Taylor, Kelly's relationship with Taylor) by not saying anything. Kelly insists that keeping the affair a secret is a better way to salvage things with Taylor than revealing the truth would be, and that this would be the best way to respect their relationships with each other and with you.

Preserving a friendship, as an end, certainly doesn't conflict with the demands of the Categorical Imperative; indeed, it seems entirely conducive to treating humanity in oneself and in one's friends as an end and not merely as a means to an end. Kant himself admits that friendship – "the union of two persons through equal mutual love and respect" – is morally important for human beings, especially insofar as it provides a context for the exercise of respect between people.[9] A moral friendship of the Kantian kind is one in which that rational respect is ultimately more important than the feelings of the participants; such friendships involve "the complete confidence of two persons in revealing their secret judgments and feelings to each other, as far as such disclosures are consistent with mutual respect."[10] Friends of this kind should be able to be entirely open with each other, an openness that includes occasional criticism motivated by the demands of duty.[11] As such, maintaining the right kinds of friendship amounts to a meritorious or imperfect duty – it improves the conditions for the exercise of morality.

Is your friendship with Kelly a properly moral friendship in which mutual respect is important? You might have thought so before you discovered Kelly's infidelity and were encouraged by Kelly to hide the truth from Taylor. In this case, though, it seems clear to you that keeping the affair secret is no better than lying outright. You would be using Taylor as a means to the end of maintaining your friendship with Kelly, which is clearly not what duty would demand. It is also apparent to you that Kelly would not have told you about the affair in the first place if you hadn't happened upon it yourself, which means that Kelly was deceiving you as well as Taylor. A friendship in which disclosures and deceits of this kind occur does not appear to be one consistent with mutual respect – Kelly is using you as a means to Kelly's own end (cheating on Taylor), and that end in itself is morally wrong.

After considering things in this light, you decide to stick to your ultimatum, but Kelly still objects. From Kelly's point of view, it looks as if you are forcing Kelly to accomplish *your* end, which would violate the Categorical Imperative. You respond by pointing out that your ultimatum is really more of a courtesy than a threat – you are giving Kelly relevant information necessary to making a choice by describing your own intended behavior. If you are committed to acting as a denizen of the Kingdom of Ends, you must act as if others, too, are bound by the same moral rules that bind you. You must act as if Kelly's will were also determined by reason, not by inclination, and reason has already discerned the wrongness of deception (not to mention the wrongness of infidelity – a classic example of the use of a person as a mere means to one's own end). You cannot promise to hide the truth from Taylor, and you will not help Kelly do so.

NOTES

[1] Immanuel Kant, *Groundwork of the Metaphysics of Morals*, in *Practical Philosophy (The Cambridge Edition of the Works of Immanuel Kant)*, Mary J. Gregor, trans. and ed., (Cambridge: Cambridg e University Press), 1996. 4:393; "good will" is in bold in the original, but I have changed the emphasis to italics here. All citations for Kant will use AK numbers.

[2] Kant, *Groundwork*, 4:412-4:413.

[3] Kant, *Groundwork*, 4:413.

[4] I say "at least three" because there are ongoing disputes among Kant scholars and translators about this number, but the broad consensus is that there are *at least* three.

[5] *Groundwork* 4:421.

[6] Kant, *Groundwork*, 4:429.

[7] Kant, *Groundwork*, 4:434-4:440

[8] Kant, *Groundwork*, 4:422-4:424.

[9] Kant, *The Metaphysics of Morals*, 6:469.

[10] Kant, *The Metaphysics of Morals*, 6:471.

[11] Kant, *The Metaphysics of Morals*, in *Practical Philosophy*, 6:469

CLASSICAL UTILITARIANISM
AND CONSEQUENTIALISM

The class of ethical positions identified in this chapter – *consequentialism* – is arguably among the most popular normative orientations in contemporary ethical theory, although it has a very long and respectable history going as far back as ancient Greece. Two of the most famous proponents of consequentialist-style normative theory are the *classical utilitarians* Jeremy Bentham (1748-1832) and John Stuart Mill (1806-1873). My presentation hereafter will focus primarily on their work, which I will use to build an elementary model for other kinds of consequentialist approach.

Consequentialism, in the broadest sense, is the view that what makes a choice morally good or bad is the set of consequences that follow from it. In other words, if a given choice leads to bad results, then the choice is morally wrong. If it leads to good results, then it is morally correct. As simple as it appears, however, any consequentialist theory must at some point develop a robust account of what constitutes a good or a bad result if it is to function as a reliable indicator of moral value. There are a number of different possible ways to offer such an account. Classical utilitarianism, for example, depends on one central assumption about human motivation: human beings are motivated by the desire to acquire pleasure or happiness and to avoid pain and suffering, for which reason what counts as a good or a bad consequence to be measured against gaining pleasure and avoiding pain. As John Stuart Mill puts it in *Utilitarianism,*

The creed which accepts as the foundation of morals "utility" or the "greatest happiness principle" holds that actions are right in proportion as they tend to promote happiness; wrong as they tend to produce the reverse of happiness. By happiness is intended pleasure and the absence of pain; by unhappiness, pain and the privation of pleasure.[1]

The *greatest happiness principle* to which Mill refers is actually a slogan of Jeremy Bentham's: "The Greatest Happiness for the Greatest Number." According to Bentham (and to both John Stuart Mill and his father James Mill, who was a utilitarian contemporary of Bentham's), utility is not satisfied by purely individual and selfish choices; maximizing one's own pleasure at the expense of everyone else's isn't good at all. The happiness that utility is meant to promote is the general happiness of all, not the narrow pleasures of individuals or small minority segments of a larger population.[2] Note that Bentham does *not* talk about the greatest happiness of the *majority*, and in fact explicitly rejects that interpretation of his slogan. Rather, what Bentham appears to mean is that the utilitarian goal is to maximize pleasure across the whole population, not merely the largest number of individual members of the population.[3] Further, no one person's happiness is any more or less important than any other person's happiness; as Mill points out, "Bentham's dictum 'everybody to count for one, nobody to count for more than one,' might be written under the principle of utility as an explanatory commentary."[4]

While all individuals are equal to each other, however, the classical utilitarians often argue that not all *pleasures* are equally valuable. Because human beings are complex rational creatures, they are capable of a very wide range of pleasures, some of which are qualitatively better than others. While it is possible for a human being to pursue a life of base pleasures (feeding, fighting, fornicating), they hold that it is better to pursue a life that includes higher-order pleasures that exercise one's capacities as a rational being more fully (a notion the utilitarians share with virtue theorists like Aristotle). "It is better," Mill tells us, "to be a human being dissatisfied than a pig satisfied; better to be Socrates dissatisfied than a fool satisfied. And if the fool, or the pig, are of a different opinion, it is because they know only their own side of the question."[5]

As elegant and straightforward as the utilitarian approach might appear, there are a few puzzles that pose some difficulty for applying it. How, for example, is a moral thinker to determine which consequences are relevant to the calculation of a choice's utility and which ones are not? Should we confine our thinking only to actual consequences, or should we also consider hypothetically possible results? Should we confine our deliberations to immediate results, or must we extend our thinking to the longest term possible? Does the requirement that each individual's concerns count equally make it difficult to differentiate among relevant and irrelevant consequences and stakeholders? There is still quite a lot of disagreement on these points (and many others), and I do not propose to settle matters here. Many later consequentialists point out that there is much more to the human good than simple pleasures and pains. The notion of human well-being or welfare must itself be just as complex as human beings are, and may include concerns that, while not obviously connected to pleasure or pain, are nonetheless vitally important. For this reason, contemporary consequentialists tend to argue in terms of broader conceptions of human welfare and harm/benefit rather than relying on the simpler utilitarian pleasure/pain calculus.

There is a further problem for consequentialists of all stripes: to what should we apply the principle of utility? If we apply the principle of utility to individual choices or actions (a position called *act utilitarianism* or *act consequentialism*), we may inadvertently miss cases in which acceptable short-term consequences are followed by very bad long-term consequences. In order to avoid that sort of situation, *rule utilitarians* (and *rule consequentialists*) believe that the principle of utility ought to be applied to *rules* for action rather than to particular actions. What is good as a rule, however, may not always be good in a given situation. It might be good, for example, to follow a rule that says that one ought always to stop the car at crosswalks, but in a situation in which stopping at just that point might lead to harm somehow (accidentally blocking an ambulance on an emergency call), going through and getting out of the way without stopping might have better consequences. I will explore the difference between rule and act utilitarianism a bit in the application example that follows.

What Choice Leads To The Best Outcome?

While virtue ethics suggests that we should think about character and Kantian-style deontological ethics aims at a choice derived from duty – all things that stand prior to your choice -- a consequentialist is more interested in what happens *after* you choose. What decision will yield the best outcome? Consequentialist moral reasoning also requires you to make some decisions about what constitutes a good or a bad outcome. For the moment, let's assume that you believe that your moral goal is to minimize or avoid harm, if possible, and to promote the happiness and well-being of everyone concerned.

Kelly has given you a choice that can have a number of likely results. If you choose not to tell Taylor and Kelly breaks off the affair without Taylor ever being any the wiser, it's possible that all could be well. No one would need to be unduly upset, and Kelly would have an opportunity to work to improve their relationship. Still, Taylor could learn of the affair later from some other source, which would cause harm to Taylor and open damage to Taylor's relationship with Kelly. If you choose not to tell Taylor and Kelly continues the affair, then you are enabling Kelly's deceptive behavior, but if Taylor never finds out, it's still possible for things to go reasonably well. Of course, experience suggests that secrets of this kind are difficult to keep. The longer the deceit continues, the more likely it is that Taylor will discover it, with or without your help. If the affair continues and Taylor discovers the truth without your assistance, things could go very badly indeed – Taylor will certainly be hurt by Kelly's behavior, and if your complicity in hiding Kelly's infidelity is uncovered, then that will cause further harm to you in the context of your relationship with Taylor. There may also be negative outcomes for Kelly and Taylor's children (especially if their parents' relationship ends in hostility and recrimination) and for the spouse and family of Kelly's coworker/fellow cheater. If you tell Taylor what you know, you run the risk of doing rather a lot of damage all at once: Kelly will be hurt, Taylor will be hurt, their relationship to each other and their respective relationships with you will be damaged, and you may also be hurt yourself.

If you approach this puzzle from the position of an act utilitarian, you will need to answer one question for yourself: is your ultimatum to Kelly the best approach you could take, or should you make a different choice (either to keep Kelly's secret or to reveal it immediately to Taylor)? It appears to you, once you consider all of the likely outcomes, that while there are no entirely harmless options for you in this case, your original ultimatum minimizes damage and promotes a happier ending. The main reason your choice to encourage Kelly to be truthful and to end the affair (and to break the news yourself if Kelly does not) is preferable to either keeping the secret or revealing it immediately is because it accomplishes two things: it minimizes the damage across the entire system that includes you as well as Taylor and Kelly and it generates a set of conditions under which Kelly and Taylor might be able to deal with their relationship issues in a way that could lead to greater happiness for them both. You believe it would be better (that is, less harmful, more conducive to happiness) if Kelly chooses to end the affair, confesses it, and then commits to working with Taylor either to repair or to end their relationship. Taylor's receiving information about the affair from you first would probably make things much worse for both of them, and it would undoubtedly cause trouble in your own interactions with them as individuals. Kelly is unlikely to come clean without the pressure of possible exposure by you. Your ultimatum tends to lead to the best result.

Kelly still disagrees, though (of course!). After all, your ultimatum certainly makes Kelly unhappy, for which reason it damages your relationship. It also, Kelly claims, will lead to much more misery than just keeping the affair secret. Taylor cannot be hurt, after all, by cheating about which Taylor does not know. If Kelly ended the affair without revealing anything and committed to the process of trying to repair the problems in their relationship that provided the incentive for infidelity, that would be ever so much better for them both in terms of minimizing misery and promoting happiness. It would also be better for you and for Kelly and Taylor's children.

In response to this objection, you change tactics and approach your dilemma from the rule-utilitarian point of view. Using that approach requires you to consider whether, as a rule, it is better to conceal infidelity or to reveal it. It occurs to you that a world in which people who discover deceptions of this kind do not reveal them is a world in which deception in general is much more likely to happen. A world in which deception is much more likely to happen seems to you to be a much more dangerous and harmful world in which people are more likely to be honest instead of deceptive – such a world might well see crimes go unpunished, as well as seeing an increase in crimes that depend on fraud and deception. It would be a world, on the whole, that is much less conducive to human happiness and well being than a world in which there are fewer incentives to deceive.

Your decision stands.

NOTES

[1] John Stuart Mill, *Utilitarianism*, in *The Classical Utilitarians: Bentham and Mill*, John Troyer, ed., (Indianapolis: Hackett Publishing Company, Inc.), 2003, 99.
[2] Jeremy Bentham, "The Greatest Good for the Greatest Number [Excerpt on the phrase 'Greatest Happiness of the Greatest Number'], in *The Classical Utilitarians: Bentham and Mill*, John Troyer, ed., (Indianapolis: Hackett Publishing Company, Inc.), 2003, 92-93.
[3] Bentham, "Greatest Good," 92.
[4] Mill, *Utilitarianism*, 144.
[5] Mill, *Utilitarianism*, 102.

THE ETHICS OF CARE

Once upon a time (the 1970s), psychologist Carol Gilligan observed some striking differences between the ways in which her male subjects expressed themselves and their judgments and the ways in which her female subjects did so. She noticed that the female subjects she studied tended to be particularly self-effacing, erasing themselves from their own assertions. She also noticed that their moral decision-making reflected a greater emphasis on complex relationships than on rights, rules, or principles. In her classic book *In A Different Voice*, she suggested the possibility that this emphasis on caring relations might represent a viable and distinct moral orientation.[1]

Gilligan's work is really descriptive rather than normative – she is, after all, a psychologist rather than a moral philosopher. Normative ethicists, however, have taken up the implications of Gilligan's psychological work. The result is a form of feminist ethics that is usually called the *ethics of care*. The position care ethicists stake out is one that stands in contrast to the normative theories described so far (Kantian deontology, utilitarianism, Aristotelian virtue ethics), although it does have a lot in common with virtue-ethical practice. In this chapter, I am going to lay out a normative care-ethical approach that pulls together some of the work of philosophers Nel Noddings and Virginia Held, both of whom attempt to systematize the observations Gilligan and others made about caring and relationships into a robust form of practical ethics.

According to Virginia Held, the many varieties of the ethics of care typically include a set of shared features. An ethic of care usually begins with a "central focus...on the compelling moral salience of attending to and meeting the needs of the particular others for whom we take responsibility," which shifts the focus of care-ethical arguments from independent individuals to interdependent systems of relation.[2] According to Held, "moralities built on the image of the independent, autonomous, rational individual largely overlook the reality of human dependence" – we spend rather a lot of our lives (as children and as adults) dependent on others *and* as persons on whom others depend.[3] In other words, the ethics of care is less about determining how isolated rational individuals ought to make decisions, and more about how beings who are necessarily connected to others should best manage those relationships. It also focuses our moral concern on *particular* others (my child, your mother, our friend, this person before us) rather than on the development of impartial judgments concerning humanity in the abstract.[4] The very emotional content that a thinker like Kant, for example, would find problematic is immensely important to an ethic of care; it is a part of our ethical job, according to Held, to consider those emotions very carefully indeed, and to develop an account of how best to evaluate and act on them.[5]

Because the ethics of care conceives of human agents always in the context of their relationships rather than as isolated individuals, all morally relevant decisions are made relationally rather than individually, and they are all personal. There are no abstractions here – only people, connected to each other in any number of degrees of intensity and complexity. One way to talk about this relational business is to take up Nel Noddings' description of moral agents in terms of their roles: the *one-caring* and the *cared-for*.[6] Working out the nature of these relationships will also make the nature of *caring* itself (in the sense relevant to the ethics of care) a bit clearer. Note that for Noddings and other care-theorists, ethical "caring" is not an emotion. Properly moral caring is an orientation and a drive toward action, not just a feeling, and it may apply even to people we don't particularly like or know well – this is the distinction between what Noddings calls *natural caring* (the care we feel for family, friends, loved ones, etc.) and *ethical caring*, in which we are obligated to receive others and relate to them regardless of the feelings that natural caring requires.[7] This distinction is important – it marks the difference between merely preferring to help someone we like and taking up the ethical work of receiving and responding to others.

For Noddings, the one-caring operates in an essentially empathetic or receptive mode; she is engaged in the practice of assuming the point of view of the cared-for and taking on the cared-for's interests and needs as her own.[8] The cared-for, in return, takes up the work of satisfying those interests and needs under the attention and with the support of the one-caring.[9] The one-caring and the cared-for are in a relationship that isn't so much *reciprocal* as it is *shared*. If the cared-for does not respond positively to the attention and aid of the one-caring, that's a fairly serious moral problem and might undermine the ability of the one-caring to be receptive, and if the one-caring does not assume the point of view of the cared-for in the right way, then the cared-for may not receive the caring action that true receptivity would generate.

One of Noddings' examples is nicely instructive on this point. She asks us to imagine a teacher who loves mathematics, and who is faced with a student who hates mathematics. The teacher, backed up by current research, may imagine that it is her job to find a way to help the student to love mathematics.[10] In so doing, her work will make her student "an object of study and manipulation" for her.[11] She is not, if that is the case, really being receptive to her student – she is not adopting the student's position, she's assuming that all would be well if she could make the student's position match her own. A truly receptive one-caring doesn't make that move. Instead, the teacher ought to imagine what it might really be like to find mathematics boring and awful, and to seek ways for the student to find his or her own motivation to study it.[12] As Noddings puts it, "apprehending the other's reality, feeling what he feels as nearly as possible, is the essential part of caring from the view of the one-caring."[13] Teacher and student, under a condition in which the teacher is receptive as one-caring, may move forward together to help the student find true motivation instead of imposing an idea of motivation from the teacher's perspective. They might begin, perhaps, with questions to the student about what the problem really is, and what the student finds inspiring or motivational or helpful.

The ethics of care, represented in the relation between the one-caring and the cared-for, is ultimately bound up in particular situations and persons. The right solution in one instance cannot be taken to be a rule for some other instance. This makes care-ethical thinking appear relativistic when compared to other views. Where other theories assert universal standards, care does not. Just the same, the ethics of care does make the broad (perhaps even universal) claim that the source of our obligations lies in relationships in the receptive mode. When a care ethicist is faced with a situation in which, for example, she is asked to choose to save one person rather than another from a burning house, she might well be expected to ask any number of questions about how she could best relate to the persons involved in her choice. It *matters*, for a care-ethical thinker, who these people are, how they got where they are, and how they are related to others. If the choice is between saving a child and an adult, the care ethicist (instead of invoking a rule that says one or the other has priority) might well take issue with the framing of the dilemma itself, which seems to demand relating to the idea of a child in general and the idea of an adult in general rather than *this particular* child and *this particular* adult.

It's necessary to keep in mind that one may be simultaneously the one-caring and the cared-for in the context of any given relationship, and is therefore bound both to receiving the other and to allowing oneself to be received and supported by the other. Just as I have been the cared-for of my mother, I may also be one-caring for her. The ethics of care also asserts that we are involved in a complex web of relations in which we may be both givers and receivers of care, and while our immediate relations are the most important, the obligation to be receptive doesn't simply disappear over distance and time.[14] We are obligated to remain open to receiving others as we encounter them.[15]

Of course, receiving others and taking up their interests does not necessarily mean agreeing with them or doing whatever they want. One-caring in a relationship with a cared-for who is self-destructive is not required to enable self-destructive choices or behaviors. The point of receptive ethical caring is to promote the continuance and growth of caring relationships, not to allow them to fall apart. That means that, for example, the one-caring may make choices that further the caring relationship, but which do not actually please the cared-for at the time (an addict's parent encouraging him to enter rehab, for example). This is an important point on which some forms of consequentialism and the ethics of care appear to differ.

What Does Care Require?

Unlike the other three normative theories studied so far, the ethics of care requires you to be most deeply concerned with the way in which Kelly's infidelity and secrecy affects the set of relationships in which those behaviors occur. While the reasoning process of the ethics of care can look quite a lot like the reasoning process found in virtue ethics, there is an important difference: as Virginia Held points out, "virtue ethics focuses especially on the states of character of individuals, whereas the ethics of care concerns itself especially with caring relations."[16] While the other theories do require you to think about how the moral law/utility/virtue might intersect with relationships, the ethics of care centers the relationships themselves as the most important element for consideration. Put another way: in the other ethical approaches studied so far, the relationships involved in this dilemma are factors for moral consideration, while for the ethics of care, they are the most important part of the problem.

You begin your deliberations by putting yourself in the position of one-caring relative to Kelly. In so doing, you adopt Kelly's point of view as your own, and consider what it might mean to adopt Kelly's choices as your own. Kelly has been with Taylor for a long time, and wants to remain with Taylor. Kelly also wants more from that relationship than Taylor is currently able to give. Kelly loves their children, and does not want to hurt anyone, including the coworker/friend-with-benefits, of whom Kelly is in fact rather fond. Kelly's position is difficult – there is at least some satisfaction to be had from pursuing the affair, but the shortcomings in the relationship between Kelly and Taylor that motivated the infidelity remain unaddressed. It hurts when one's needs and one's partner's needs are incompatible. It is also hard to keep secrets from the people one loves. Kelly likes and respects you, and does not want to lose your good opinion. Curiously, the very things that motivate Kelly to lie and endanger a whole set of relationships are urges that naturally flow from a desire to keep those same relationships intact (an instance of natural caring, rather than ethical caring). As one-caring, you cannot ignore this fact.

Yet, as one-caring for Taylor, you cannot ignore the hurt Taylor would feel upon discovery of Kelly's infidelity. You also cannot ignore the fact that Kelly's infidelity exists in the context of a relationship with Taylor that is currently under considerable strain -- a strain the entire nature of which, apparently, Taylor may not know. Taylor might be blissfully unaware now, but there's no guarantee that the secret will be kept even if you personally hold your peace, and Taylor would certainly be devastated. The other relationships that seem to have bearing on this problem also move you – Taylor and Kelly's children, Kelly's co-worker and the co-worker's spouse –

in large part because they are connected to Taylor and Kelly (to whom you are more directly related).

Your priority, in the practice of care, is to maintain all of these relationships and, if possible, to help them to flourish and grow. But how? You understand why Kelly has been unfaithful, and why Kelly is asking you to keep it secret. You understand Kelly's fellow cheater's motivations in the same way. You know, however, that Taylor would be terribly hurt to discover the deception, and that Kelly and Taylor's current relationship is deeply wounded. While continuing the deception for Kelly's sake might cause less short-term stress and immediate hurt for Kelly and Kelly's co-worker, and while it might not add to Taylor's unhappiness so long as the secret is never revealed, the fact that Kelly and Taylor's relationship is already hurting weighs heavily in your considerations. Kelly's infidelity is a symptom of a sickness that needs healing, and you would not be truly receptive either to Kelly or to Taylor if you didn't make that fact the central issue in your deliberations. While it might do you some hurt, as one-caring, if either or both of them ceased (as ones cared-for) to trust you, you could not exercise proper ethical care by simply pretending you don't know or lying about it. A relationship infected with deception is not a healthy one, and it cannot flourish properly – you cannot act as one-caring with a cared-for whose condition is deliberately hidden from you, and you likewise cannot be truly receptive to someone while still keeping from that person information vital to their well-being. Asking for trust while simultaneously betraying it is not true ethical caring.

Jumping straight into the fray and telling Taylor outright, however, doesn't seem to you to be the best way to address either Taylor's or Kelly's needs in this complex set of relationships. While you do not agree with Kelly's choices, you do understand their motivation, and you do not believe that dropping a bomb in the middle of an already troubled relationship will be good for the kind of healing that relationship requires. Kelly and Taylor's relationship is, after all, *theirs*, not yours. You can receive them both, you can put yourself in the position of supporting them, but you cannot do for them what must be done in order to save their relationship. All you can do is try to make the actions they need to take in order to heal possible. Just as the teacher could not be truly receptive by trying to manipulate the student into loving mathematics, you cannot truly be engaged in ethical care by interfering too much with Taylor and Kelly's choices.

Your ultimatum still seems to you, given all of these considerations, to be a fair choice, mostly because it provides a motivation for Kelly to try to do the work of fixing things with Taylor and respects their own investments in each other and in others. Yet, as Kelly correctly points out, your ultimatum amounts to a kind of manipulation, wherein you pressure Kelly to do the right thing. This too seems to be a failure of receptivity, an imposition of yourself on the other rather than an adoption of the other's experience and interests.

The only other choice that might be appropriate, as far as you can tell, is to find some other way to encourage Kelly to find personal reasons to end the affair, to confess it, and to work on mending things with Taylor. The key point, as far as you're concerned, is that you need to help Kelly (already cared-for by you) to act as one-caring relative to Taylor. In the receptive mode of one-caring, Kelly might be more likely to make the kinds of decisions that will be conducive to repairing and maintaining relationships.

It's time, you think, for a much longer conversation, one in which you listen rather a lot more than you talk and try to assist in the connection of Kelly's needs as one cared-for to Kelly's capacity to be one-caring. That conversation should certainly include finding a way for Kelly to be receptive to Taylor, but also to Kelly's coworker/fellow cheater, to Taylor and Kelly's children, and to you.

NOTES

[1] Carol Gilligan, *In A Different Voice: Psychological Theory and Women's Development*, (Cambridge: Harvard University Press), 1993, xiii.

[2] Virginia Held, *The Ethics of Care: Personal, Political, and Global*, (New York: Oxford University Press, Inc.), 2006, 10.

[3] Held, *The Ethics of Care*, 10.

[4] Held, *The Ethics of Care*, 11

[5] Held, *The Ethics of Care*, 11.

[6] Nel Noddings, *Caring: A Feminine Approach to Ethics & Moral Education*, (Berkeley: University of California Press), 1984, 9-29.

[7] Noddings, *Caring*, 79-80

[8] Noddings, *Caring*, 16.

[9] Noddings, *Caring*, 19-21.

[10] Noddings, *Caring*, 15.

[11] Noddings, *Caring*, 15.

[12] Noddings, *Caring*, 15.

[13] Noddings, *Caring*, 16.

[14] This is certainly true for both Noddings and Held.

[15] Noddings, *Caring*, 81-90.

[16] Held, *The Ethics of Care*, 19.

PART 2: EXAMPLES AND EXERCISES

ARGUING BY EXAMPLE: A CASE STUDY MODEL

Case study work is an important part of applied or practical ethics. For people working in disciplines outside of philosophy (in the professions of law or medicine or engineering, for example), case studies are a fairly usual way of presenting and working out professional behavioral norms and solving difficult procedural problems. For philosophers, case studies are important because they are one of the most effective ways to ground theory in practice. Grounding theory in practice is useful not only for coming up with good practical solutions to moral problems, but also for improving our normative theories in the light of experience.

In the previous chapters, I've used a single, relatively simple case in order to demonstrate how to use a normative theory to shape one's reasoning about a moral problem. In this final chapter, I do the same thing on a somewhat grander scale, this time using two of the theoretical perspectives already studied in order to offer solutions to a more complex case.

There are two fundamental steps in developing a case study for the purpose of philosophical analysis: writing up the relevant details of the case and using normative theory (or theories) to construct an argument in support of a claim about that case. Case studies may be fictional or derived from actual events. A good case study may either describe a situation that has already been resolved in some way or it may present an open-ended situation in which a choice remains to be made and justified. The story about Kelly and Taylor that I used in the previous chapters was entirely fictional, and it was open-ended (which means that it required both a choice and a justification). In this chapter, I use a real-life case (the appeal of a wrongful termination lawsuit) in which a choice has already been made.

There are a few different kinds of arguments one might make about a case study. If the incident described in the case is already over and done with, and there are no new choices to be made, then the sort of argument one makes about it will have to do with whether or not the choices in question are morally correct. If the case presented is open-ended, then the sort of argument one makes about it will involve identifying and arguing in support of a solution to the problem the case presents.

A good argument about a case study, regardless of whether it is finished or open-ended, should always take objections into account. In the chapters above, I've demonstrated how to do this on a small scale, mostly by pointing out common criticisms of the applied arguments at hand. In this chapter, I will occasionally move beyond the basic criticisms of the theories themselves and into the realm of arguments about the advantages and disadvantages of certain approaches to problems.

Because the case I use poses both a moral and a legal problem, there will actually be two different arguments presented here – one about the original situation that prompted legal action and another about the ethical issues raised by the legal action itself. I do not dispute the legal arguments presented on legal grounds. I am mounting a model of a kind of *ethical* argument, not an argument about a point of law. While points of law will certainly be relevant to the ethical case I'm going to lay out, they are not the point of the argument, and they are not the source of its most important supporting premises. It is possible for something to be entirely legal and nonetheless be immoral. In this case, I am not asserting that there was any deliberately unethical behavior on the part of the courts – I am only suggesting that *the decision itself* may be unethical when judged by the standards of a normative theory.

It is worth mentioning here that there is also a kind of ethical tension to be found in using someone else's story as an example in this way. While the events that occurred in the case I discuss in this chapter are a matter of public record, some of the more personal-seeming commentary occasioned by the attempt to apply the ethics of care to the situation are potentially intrusive speculations that (ironically) might not themselves pass the test of a care-ethical approach to dealing with the problem. One way to avoid conflicts like this in case study work is to build fictionalized versions of actual events, appropriately disguising the names of the participants in order give them some privacy and to spare them the intrusion.

Sex Discrimination or Marital Salvation?

Melissa Nelson worked as a dental assistant in the office of James H. Knight, DDS for a little more than ten years; by all accounts, she was good at her job and a valuable employee of the practice. During the last year and a half of her employment, Dr. Knight's behavior apparently changed in some ways that she found disturbing. He began to inform Nelson "that her clothing was too tight and revealing."[1] He made several comments about how distracting he found her appearance. They began texting each other (often to chat about their children and other personal issues), and occasionally Dr. Knight's texts were inappropriately sexual in nature; Nelson did not respond to those, although she did continue to engage in text conversations with Dr. Knight on other subjects.[2]

Other women working in the practice (including Dr. Knight's wife, Jeanne) found their relationship troubling, and they reportedly did not get along as well with Nelson. When Jeanne Knight discovered that her husband was texting Nelson, she insisted that Nelson was a threat to their marriage and demanded that he fire her immediately.[3] Dr. Knight called Nelson into a meeting in his office. With a pastor from his church present as a witness, Dr. Knight informed Nelson that he was firing her because of the threat she posed to his marriage and handed her an envelope containing one month's severance pay.[4] When Dr. Knight later met with Nelson's husband Steve (again in the company of a pastor), he said that Melissa Nelson "had not done anything wrong or inappropriate, and that she was the best dental assistant he ever had."[5] Dr. Knight added, however, that he was worried about his own responses to her, and that while there was nothing between them, "he feared he would try to have an affair with her down the road if he did not fire her."[6] Melissa Nelson's replacement was another woman; "Historically, all of [Dr. Knight's] assistants have been women."[7]

Melissa Nelson was employed in Iowa, which is an "employment-at-will" state. This means that "an employer or employee may terminate the relationship at any time, for any reason, or for no reason at all."[8] No notice prior to termination is required. There are, however, some legal limits to at-will employment. Whistleblowers, employees who are fired for complying with applicable regulations, and employees fired in violation of state and federal civil rights law may have legally actionable claims against their employers.[9] Melissa Nelson filed a complaint with the Iowa Civil Rights Commission and was granted the right to sue on the grounds that she was "discriminated against...on the basis of sex."[10] Nelson did not file a sexual harassment claim – she sued only for wrongful termination due to sex-based discrimination.[11] Nelson's main argument was that her firing amounted to sex discrimination because the threat she allegedly posed to

Dr. Knight's marriage would never have existed if she were not a woman.[12]

The district court granted Dr. Knight's motion for a summary judgment in his favor, and held that Nelson was fired because she posed a threat to Knight's marriage, not because of her sex.[13] The Iowa Supreme Court considered Nelson's appeal and later reconsidered its own judgment in that appeal, and came to the conclusion that the district court's decision had been correct. The reasoning in support of this affirmation of the lower court's decision depended on what Chief Justice Cady, in his special concurrence, described as

> the general legal principle that an adverse employment consequence experienced by an employee because of a voluntary, romantic relationship does not form the basis of a sex-discrimination suit.[14]

While Melissa Nelson and Dr. Knight did not actually have a romantic relationship, Cady asserted that the existing precedents on the matter support the contention that "when employees are terminated due to consensual, romantic or sexually suggestive relationships," no sex discrimination is occurring, largely "because the adverse employment consequence is based on sexual activity, not gender."[15]

Because Nelson was fired for her relationship with Knight, rather than for her gender as such, Cady affirmed the court's judgment that there was no ground in the law for a sex discrimination claim in this case. While Cady did admit that the fact that the relationship between Nelson was not actually sexually intimate marked Nelson's case as different from the cases used to establish the legal precedent upon which the court's affirmation depended, he argued that the lack of sexual intimacy did not "shift this case into the line of gender-discrimination cases that protect women based on their physical appearance," which was the legal support for Nelson's claim.[16] It is also worthy of note here that (as Justice Mansfield wrote in the Iowa Supreme Court's main affirmation) the scope of this decision was specifically limited by the court. Because Nelson "did not bring a sexual harassment or hostile work environment claim," the court asserted that its decision could not be read as presenting a resolution to any claim of that kind, and further that no civil rights laws had been violated.[17]

Analysis and Argument

There are two different sets of moral problems to address in this case. The first is whether or not Dr. Knight acted rightly in firing Melissa Nelson. The second is whether or not the decision of the court is morally correct. Let's use the ethics of care to think about the relationship between Nelson and Knight and consequentialism for the legal decision's implications. I will present an argument that the ethics of care suggests that Knight's decision was not the best choice available. I will also offer a consequentialist argument that while this decision is not intended to set precedent, it still has negative effects that extend beyond the scope of the case itself, which constitutes an ethical problem. Note that neither of these arguments is intended to be definitive – there are faults in each one that it is worthwhile for a student to pick out and use as points worthy of objection.

Fractured Relationships Along The Fault-line of Gender

The firing of Melissa Nelson is an interesting case for the ethics of care (note the similarities to our sample dilemma about Kelly and Taylor). What might have happened if, for example, all of the people involved had acted as ones-caring toward each other? How should they have acted as ones cared-for?

Dr. Knight certainly was *not* acting as one-caring toward Nelson or anyone else. By his own account, he was ultimately more interested in his own feelings and needs than in hers (or, for that matter, in his wife's or anyone else's). He spent quite a lot of effort trying to get her to change her clothing and behavior in order to make it easier for him to manage his own feelings. He texted her and made inappropriate comments in person, without any apparent concern over whether or not the inappropriate comments would cause her discomfort. When he was confronted by his wife, he made a choice to preserve his relationship with her by terminating his relationship with Nelson, without (as far as we know) conceding much about what really might be wrong with his own behavior; firing Nelson and admitting to her husband that she was blameless while he (Knight) was not seems to have been the full extent of his recognition of his own responsibility in that situation. Dr. Knight was not, in short, a shining example of someone acting in the receptive mode required by the ethics of care when it came to Melissa Nelson (or, again, to his wife). He also seems to have spared very little concern for his other employees and for Nelson's husband and family until after his wife confronted him.

If one of the most important priorities of the ethics of care is the promotion and maintenance of morally caring relationships, then Dr. Knight's choice to fire Melissa Nelson represents a kind of moral failing on his part. The obvious threat to Dr. Knight's marriage is Dr. Knight himself, largely because of his own unwillingness to govern his own behavior in such a way as to avoid putting both his wife and his other employees (Nelson included) in a difficult position. An attraction that exists is not therefore an attraction that must be acted on, after all. Because he singled Nelson out at work and treated her differently from his other employees, he created conditions under which the whole complex of relationships in his office was put under considerable stress. Not only did Nelson have to deal with the occasionally unwelcome behavior of her employer, she was also subjected to the distrust and dislike of her coworkers (in response to which she ironically turned to her employer for support). Jeanne Knight would not have found her husband's texting so troubling if she had not already spent more than a year observing behavior in the office that made her suspicions entirely reasonable. This put Dr. Knight in the position of sacrificing one relationship for another in a way that was damaging to both.

In addition to demonstrating fairly poor judgment and a failure of receptivity as one-caring, Dr. Knight also failed as one cared-for. Not only did he not put himself in the place of the various others in his life, he did not respond appropriately to their support and care. He treated Nelson's friendly responses to him as encouragement for a sexual relationship that she did not wish to pursue with him. While firing Nelson did give him the opportunity to repair his relationship with his wife, one cannot imagine that merely firing the object of his illicit and unwanted affections before he could act on them would entirely correct the core problem in that relationship.

Melissa Nelson, for her own part, could not have failed to notice the tensions existing between her and her fellow employees, although she seems to have misunderstood the source of their hostility. While she admitted in her court filing that some of Dr. Knight's behavior struck her as unfair, she did not do anything to correct that behavior; one imagines, given her testimony, that she found herself caught between the knowledge that certain things probably should not have been happening as they were and a desire to maintain a relationship that she valued very highly.[18] Because their relationship had been essentially innocuous for most of the decade of her employment in Dr. Knight's office, she may well have discounted her concerns about his behavior during that final year and a half as unfounded.[19] It is also possible that this explains her unwillingness to claim that his behavior amounted to a form of sexual harassment (although one can imagine making a clear case that he was in fact creating a hostile work environment). She had been, perhaps, in the position of one cared-for who did not recognize that her response to Dr. Knight as one-caring did not actually match what he was doing. She behaved as if he were morally receptive when he was not.

Jeanne Knight, in asking her husband to fire Melissa Nelson, complained not only that Nelson was flirting and wearing inappropriate clothing, but also that Nelson was "cold" to her personally.[20] If we take both Jeanne Knight and Melissa Nelson at their respective words, then there appears to be an interesting disconnect between how Nelson perceived her own behavior and how Jeanne Knight saw it. Jeanne Knight, too, seems to have been a cared-for (relative to her husband) who was not connected as she ought to have been to a proper one-caring. It's fairly clear from all of the available descriptions of Dr. Knight's behavior that he did not allow the thought that he might be harming his relationship with his wife to interfere with his unreciprocated sexual interest in Melissa Nelson until Jeanne Knight herself raised the issue with him. This is indicative of a moral failing within the marital relationship that existed over and above the "threat" posed by Melissa Nelson. Had he been one-caring for his wife, he would not have been pursuing his married assistant.

What should Dr. Knight have done? Ideally, he should have acted as one-caring from the beginning, neither imposing his attraction on Nelson nor alienating his wife and his other employees. Having already erred, though, it's not clear whether or not firing Nelson was the best decision. On the one hand, once his wife confronted him, he could have confessed his errors and begun a frank discussion with her about their marriage, perhaps with their pastor's assistance. He could also have spoken to Nelson (in the company of the pastor and/or his wife and/or Nelson's husband) about how best to proceed with her continued employment, as their relationship simply could not go on as it had. It would be wrong to hold Nelson responsible for Knight's choices and behaviors, but it would also be wrong to suddenly change the nature of their relationship without letting her understand why it had to change. She might have chosen to quit at the end of such a conversation, but that would still have been better for her sake (which is what one-caring ought to be thinking about) than firing her for something over which she ultimately had very little control.

On the other hand, refusing his wife's request to fire Nelson might only have compounded the problems both in the office and at home. Jeanne Knight might well have good reason to be suspicious of any attempt on her husband's part to keep Nelson around, given his admitted attraction to her. Taking these concerns seriously might require Nelson's firing as the only way to assure Jeanne Knight of being truly received in care. It's entirely possible that this is precisely the sort of advice that the Knights' pastor gave them, and it might explain the pastor's presence in Knight's meeting with Nelson and with Nelson's husband. The problem is that maintaining the marriage did material harm to Nelson, above and beyond any relationship she might have had with Dr. Knight: it took her employment from her, which could have been economically ruinous to her family if she were unable to find further employment in a reasonable amount of time. As one cared-for, Nelson was as ill-served here as Jeanne Knight.

The upshot of all of these considerations is that the case of Nelson v. Knight is a moral disaster from start to finish where the ethics of care is concerned.

Unfortunate Consequences

While the decision of the court in Melissa Nelson's lawsuit may not be *legally* objectionable, it is possible that the result is *ethically* problematic when considered from a consequentialist point of view. The key question is this: what are the consequences that this decision might have for employment practices and civil rights law in the State of Iowa?

The Iowa Supreme Court's affirmation of the decision to reject Nelson's claim rests largely on the argument that it was Nelson's behavior and not her identity that resulted in her firing – that is, the threat she posed to Knight's marriage resulted from the relationship she had with him rather than from the fact that she happens to be a woman. Had she been fired for being a woman, that would have violated federal and state civil rights laws, but being fired for engaging in a (non-sexual) relationship did not violate those laws. Had the relationship in question not been consensual – if it had in fact been a documented case of sexual harassment – Nelson would have had a better case for claiming that there had been a civil rights violation, albeit one of the different kind.

It is telling that the court waved off one rather significant argument from Nelson's lawyers: "if Dr. Knight would have been liable to Nelson for sexually harassing her, he should not be able to avoid liability for terminating her out of fear that he was *going* to harass her."[21] The court responded by pointing out that because sexual harassment is defined largely in terms of the existence of a hostile work environment, the absence of a claim that such an environment existed in this case meant that Nelson's claim still didn't constitute a violation of civil rights law. While the court's argument was legally correct – Nelson never did claim that a hostile work environment actually existed – there is still reason to believe that the consequence of allowing an employer to fire an employee in order to avoid a possible future misdeed on the employer's part is problematic.

There are a few different problems here, but the most troubling one is this: One consequence of permitting such a practice to stand is a legal framework in which a racist employer (for example) can deny employment to someone in a way motivated by that racism, and yet still claim that doing so is not a violation of civil rights law. All the employer has to do is make the case that the refusal to hire or to keep that employee is motivated by a desire to avoid future racist behavior on his or her own part. It allows someone to engage in a wrong action that is then justified as an attempt to avoid engaging in that very sort of action. This is both unjust and, frankly, absurd. It amounts to making the victim of wrongful behavior against which civil rights protections would otherwise operate accountable for being victimized, without ever holding the actual agent of that behavior responsible for engaging in it. The only protection that exists against this eventuality is the court's refusal to acknowledge the Nelson case as a legal precedent for arguments of this kind, and that protection is only as strong as the decision of some future court to stand by it. This is not a very reassuring outcome.

The court's argument that Nelson's gender identity was not really implicated in her firing (which allows the court to claim that this decision does not stand as a sexual harassment precedent) is also less convincing than it appears. While all of Dr. Knight's employees were women (which is why the court found it plausible to focus on the particular relationship he had with Nelson and not on her gender) that doesn't necessarily have the effect of making Nelson's firing a matter of something other than her gender. It is possible, after all, for a man to choose to discriminate against one woman and not all of the women with whom he interacts; a man who gropes his personal assistant against her wishes may nonetheless be a polite son to his mother and a perfectly appropriate brother-in-law. Just as serial killers are not made innocent by their failure to kill every person who crosses their path, the behavior of a person who commits sexual harassment or engages in gender discrimination is not any less discriminatory because he may fail to trouble every single woman he knows. If the court's notion that an employer is inoculated against accusations of sexism or gender discrimination because he does not treat *all* of his employees of the same gender identity badly goes unchallenged, then the door remains open for instances in which there are in fact civil rights violations being committed against particular individuals in a context in which the same violations are not committed against others. This effectively undermines the scope of civil rights protections, which is definitely an undesirable outcome for a just society.

NOTES

[1] *Melissa Nelson v. James H. Knight, DDS, P.C. and James Knight.* IA 11-1857 (2013) 3. Accessed via the Iowa Supreme Court's archive of recent opinions at:
http://www.iowacourts.gov/About_the_Courts/Supreme_Court/Supreme_Court_Opinions/Recent_Opinions/20130712/11-1857.pdf

[2] *Nelson v. Knight* 4 He asked her how often she experienced orgasm, among other things (see case footnote).

[3] *Nelson v. Knight* 4.

[4] *Nelson v. Knight* 5.

[5] *Nelson v. Knight* 5.

[6] *Nelson v. Knight* 5.

[7] *Nelson v. Knight* 5.

[8] "Iowa Division of Labor Wage FAQs" Question 13 .
http://www.iowaworkforce.org/labor/wagefaqs.pdf

[9] IA Division of Labor Wage FAQs Question 13.

[10] *Nelson v. Knight* 5.

[11] *Nelson v. Knight* 5-6

[12] *Nelson v. Knight* 5-6

[13] *Nelson v. Knight* 5

[14] *Nelson v. Knight.* 22.

[15] *Nelson v. Knight* 22.

[16] *Nelson v. Knight* 28.

[17] *Nelson v. Knight* 2.

[18] According to the brief, "Nelson considered Dr. Knight to be a friend and father figure, and she denies that she ever flirted with him or sought an intimate or sexual relationship with him." *Nelson v. Knight.* 3.

[19] *Nelson v. Knight.* 3.

[20] *Nelson v. Knight.* 3.

[21] *Nelson v. Knight* 13.

INTRODUCTION TO THE EXERCISES

In the pages that follow, I describe four different cases involving a set of different ethical concerns: social media and law enforcement, intellectual freedom, humane legislation related to puppy mills, and dual roles/conflicts of interest in the caring professions. Three are fictional or fictionalized, and one is drawn from an actual news story. After each case is presented, there will be a set of exercises and questions for the reader.

The basic format of the exercises is drawn from the material on arguments, objections, and methods described in the introduction (p. 7-9). For each case, you will be asked to provide a clear description of the main ethical issues involved, identify the applicable elements of each of the normative theories discussed in this book, develop a basic argument or two based on those theories, and work on some objections.

The exercises are set up to provide students with the opportunity to practice thinking and arguing about the material. There are no "right" answers given in the text or provided to the instructor – my expectation here is that students will take advantage of this chance to discuss their solutions and arguments with each other and work out a number of different approaches to the problems at hand. Have fun with it! Explore the ideas you've read here and see where they take you!

Case 1: Social Media and the Law

In October 2014, media site BuzzFeed broke a disturbing story about identity theft on Facebook. According to BuzzFeed news reporter Chris Hamby, the Drug Enforcement Agency (DEA) had created a fake profile in the name of a woman who had been arrested on drug charges, using pictures taken from her confiscated mobile phone.[1] DEA agent Timothy Sinnigen set up the fake profile to be used in a sting aimed at catching the "ringleader" of the drug gang with which this woman was allegedly affiliated. According to *The Washington Post*,

> "Sinnigen posted photographs from [Prince's] phone, to which he had been granted access, to the undercover Facebook page," an August court filing by the government states. "… Defendants admit [Prince] did not give express permission for the use of the photographs contained on her phone on an undercover Facebook page, but state [that Prince] implicitly consented by granting access to the information stored in her phone." […] All the pics were fair game. Even ones showing Prince scantily dressed, which [Sinnigen] used in the fake profile. "Defendants admit that in one photograph of [Prince] that was used on the undercover Facebook page, [she] was wearing either a two-piece bathing suit or a bra and underwear," the filing states.[2]

The woman whose identity was stolen (Sondra Prince, AKA Sondra Arquiett) had no knowledge of what Sinnigen had been doing with her image and identity for three months, during which time he used the profile to contact at least one known drug dealer. Prince sued the DEA and Sinnigen in October 2014, and in January 2015 a Federal court supervised a mediation process that led to a settlement awarding Prince $134,000 in damages (a settlement in which, it should be noted, the government did not admit any wrongdoing).[3]

While the government claimed that creating fake social media profiles for the purpose of investigative work was neither unusual nor illegal, Facebook also sent a letter of complaint to the DEA, asking them to stop engaging in the practice. According to the letter, the creation of fake profiles does in fact violate the Facebook Terms of Service to which all users must agree, as well as undermining the trust necessary for the community of Facebook users to function.[4]

Exercises

1. Identify the central ethical problem and then briefly describe the ethically relevant details of this case. [Hint: think about privacy...]

2. For each of the normative theories you've studied so far, briefly describe how the theory might address the problem and details you describe in (1). Your goal in this task is to pick out a claim that you can treat as the conclusion of an ethical argument either for or against the DEA agent's behavior.

3. Come up with two arguments – one *for* the DEA and one *against* – using any of the normative theories you've studied so far. Present each argument as a list of ordered premises leading to a conclusion (use the simple model on p. 6 for guidance).

4. Come up with at least one good objection to each of your proposed arguments. Explain why you think it is a good objection.

5. Respond to the objections – that is, imagine how you might defend each argument by changing a premise, undermining the premises of the objection, etc.

6. Discussion questions: What difference (if any) would the following hypothetical changes in circumstance make to your judgment about whether or not the DEA agent did something unethical? Explain.
   a. Instead of being revealing, Ms. Prince's pictures were nondescript, modest, and unintrusive.
   b. Instead of using Ms. Prince's images and content, the DEA agent only used her name and some stock images from a public domain photo site.
   c. Instead of cloning Ms. Prince's account, the DEA agent acquired her password as a part of a legal search and used her actual Facebook account for the same purpose.
   d. Instead of being a known drug user, Ms. Prince was an entirely innocent person who happened to be in the wrong place at the wrong time.

NOTES

[1] Hamby, Chris. "Government Set Up A Fake Facebook Page In This Woman's Name." *BuzzFeed.* October 6, 2014. https://www.buzzfeed.com/chrishamby/government-says-federal-agents-can-impersonate-woman-online?utm_term=.qsvJJl5dBv#.pnqJJLZ1r3 .

[2] McCoy, Terence. "DEA created a fake Facebook profile in this woman's name using seized pics — then impersonated her." October 7, 2014.
https://www.washingtonpost.com/news/morning-mix/wp/2014/10/07/dea-created-a-fake-facebook-profile-in-this-womans-name-using-seized-pics-then-impersonated-her/ .

[3] Lyons, Brendan J. "Feds pay $134,000 to settle DEA agent's fake Facebook case." *Albany Times Union.* January 20, 2015. http://www.timesunion.com/news/article/Feds-pay-134k-to-woman-whose-ID-used-by-DEA-on-6027904.php . The actual settlement agreement can be found here: http://msnbcmedia.msn.com/i/MSNBC/Sections/NEWS/AJDocs/150120-Arquiett-Facebook-Settlement.pdf

[4] Pagliery, Jose. "Facebook tells DEA: Stop impersonating users." *CNNMoney.* December 9, 2014. http://money.cnn.com/2014/10/20/technology/security/facebook-dea/ . Read the complaint letter here: http://i.cdn.turner.com/money/2014/images/10/20/facebook-letter-to-dea.pdf?iid=EL .

Theory and Practice

Case 2: Freedom and Judgment

Kristie Kidder is the director of the Botham Regional Library. She does her very best to make BRL a welcoming place for the people in her community, which is sometimes pretty challenging -- the Botham population is large and wildly varied, and there are some serious disagreements among members of the community about which materials ought to be in the library's collection. She arrived at her office this morning to discover several angry phone messages and emails waiting for her, all concerning the new book announcements: apparently, some people are furious that the library now owns a copy of famous local supervillain The Giggler's new book *A Manual for Mayhem: Putting a Rictus Grin On The Face of America.*

The people protesting the acquisition say that the book is dangerous -- it does in fact include instructions for doing violent and destructive things, and it is a book intentionally written to promote villainous behavior up to and including the overthrow of governments. They also believe that it is especially risky to have this book in a library that serves young people, because children may not be able to exercise appropriate judgment about the content of the text and what it recommends. The protesters' main demand is that the library remove this book from the collection, as a service to the taxpayers. They would also like the library to institute a collection development policy that would prohibit the purchase of books and other materials with "dangerous" content.

Yet, in accord with the American Library Association's ethical guidelines, Director Kidder and her acquisitions staff are also professionally bound to refuse the protestors' request. One of the ALA's core ethical principles is the protection of intellectual freedom, which includes a commitment to "[resisting] all efforts to censor library resources."[1] Both the removal of this particular book and the development of a special collection development policy that would prevent the purchase of other books of the kind appear to constitute forms of censorship.

What should Director Kidder do?

Exercises

1. Identify the central ethical problem and then briefly describe the ethically relevant details of this case. Which values or ethical commitments are in conflict with each other here?

2. For each of the normative theories you've studied so far, briefly describe how the theory might address the problem and details you describe in (1). Your goal in this task is to pick out a claim that you can treat as the conclusion of an ethical argument either for or against some possible solution to Director Kidder's problem.

3. Come up with a solution to Director Kidder's problem – what should she do? Should she give in to the protesters or refuse? Present your argument as a list of ordered premises leading to a conclusion (use the simple model on p. 6 for guidance).

4. Come up with at least two good objections to your proposed argument. Explain why you think it they are good objections.

5. Respond to the objections – that is, imagine how you might defend your argument by changing a premise, undermining the premises of the objection, etc.

6. Discussion questions: What difference (if any) would the following hypothetical changes in circumstance make to your judgment about what Director Kidder ought to do? Explain.
    a. The protesters are instead calling for the removal of the entire *Harry Potter* series from the collection because it might mislead children into thinking that magic is not sinful and that witchcraft is good.
    b. Instead of running a public library, Director Kidder is running the library at a small private religious college with a required statement of faith and code of conduct for all employees.
    c. The protesters are instead calling for the removal of all religious texts from the public library, on the grounds that a public institution funded by the local government should not promote religion.
    d. Instead of running a public library, Kristie Kidder is the administrator responsible for selecting materials for the library at a state prison.

NOTES

[1] The American Library Association's Code of Ethics can be read here: http://www.ala.org/advocacy/proethics/codeofethics/codeethics

Case 3: Puppy Farming

Puppies sold at pet stores in the United States typically come from USDA-licensed farmers (sometimes called "puppy mills") who raise the dogs just as they would raise hogs, sheep, or cattle -- that is, the dogs are treated as livestock, and are kept under conditions that allow the maximum number to be bred at the lowest cost (and therefore the highest potential profit). What that means, in practice, is this:

> 1) There is no genetic testing done for inherited defects like hip dysplasia, luxating patella, congenital deafness, and other conditions with symptoms that often do not manifest until the dog is physically mature; mass-bred puppies are usually shipped to stores as soon after they are weaned as possible. Pups deemed visibly defective at birth are culled (euthanized) rather than sold.

> 2) Because the goal of the breeding operation is to produce a large volume of sale-worthy pups at low cost, breeders of this kind usually do not engage in the time-consuming and expensive work of training and working the dogs or selecting very carefully over the long term for good conformation and good temperament in their stock.

Advocates for animal welfare who wish to shut down the puppy mills claim that these puppy farming operations are inhumane. They would rather see people adopt shelter dogs than perpetuate the dog overpopulation problem by buying mill-produced dogs. The farmers, however, claim that they are running perfectly reasonable livestock operations, and that people ought to have the right to purchase a dog as they see fit. Farmers of other kinds of livestock further claim that the animal welfare activists are trying to shut down their livelihood. These other farmers argue that regulations for farmed dogs would extend to cattle, hogs, sheep, and poultry, in ways that would make it impossible to raise these animals for meat consumption.

The state of Iowa is one of several Midwest states in which people are trying to create better legislation for dog-breeding operations. What should the state of Iowa do about puppy mills?

Exercises

1. Identify the central ethical problem(s) and then briefly describe the ethically relevant details of this case.

2. For each of the normative theories you've studied so far, briefly describe how the theory might address the problem and details you describe in (1). Your goal in this task is to pick out a claim that you can treat as the conclusion of an ethical argument either for or against the practice of raising dogs as livestock.

3. Come up with two arguments – one *for* the puppy mill production model and one *against* – using any of the normative theories you've studied so far. Present each argument as a list of ordered premises leading to a conclusion (use the simple model on p. 6 for guidance).

4. Come up with at least one good objection to each of your proposed arguments. Explain why you think it is a good objection.

5. Respond to the objections – that is, imagine how you might defend each argument by changing a premise, undermining the premises of the objection, etc.

6. Discussion questions: What difference (if any) would the following hypothetical changes in circumstance make to your judgment about whether or not the practice of farming dogs is unethical? Explain.
   a. Scholars present evidence that dogs are cognitively different from cattle – they are psychologically harmed by conditions that otherwise wouldn't bother steer.
   b. Studies appear to show that culling prior to sale (euthanizing unhealthy pups) can be shown to catch many or most health problems; there is no significant difference between the health of mill-bred purebred dogs and mutts.
   c. PETA has managed successfully to lobby for legislation in Iowa that would make the rules for puppy mills apply to hog confinements.

Case 4: A Conflict of Interest

Therapists and counselors are, in the course of their work, privy to private, personal information provided by their clients. Because the therapeutic relationship is built on a guarantee of confidentiality, clients are supposed to feel free to reveal things to the therapist that it might be quite awkward or even harmful for them to discuss openly in other contexts. Because the therapist has privileged access to such information, it becomes possible for therapist and client to develop treatment plans that specifically address the client's actual needs in an environment of trust and care.

One of the ethical risks involved in therapeutic settings is the difficulty posed by various kinds of *dual relationships* – that is, those cases in which counselor and client may also be related to each other in some other way (as co-workers, as relatives, as friends, as teachers and students, as fellow residents of a community, etc.). While sexual relationships between clients and therapists are strictly forbidden, other sorts of relationships often fall into a bit of a gray area, and can represent a conflict of interest.

Dr. Lukas is the new staff counselor at Thunder River Junior College in the small town of Thunder River, North Dakota. Thunder River is a small, isolated rural community of about 10,000 people, and the college enrolls roughly 1,000 students who come mostly from the town and surrounding communities. Dr. Lukas is helping Michaela, a student at the college, deal with stress and anxiety issues. After several weeks of therapy, Michaela tells him that she is having trouble with her current boyfriend; she is worried that he seems to be emotionally manipulative in a way that might become abusive. When asked to say more about it, she is reluctant to speak, but eventually reveals that she is dating one of the college faculty.

This poses a difficulty. Michaela is a competent adult and not a dependent, and there is nothing about the relationship (no physical evidence of domestic violence, etc.) that would legally require Dr. Lukas to report it to the authorities. The college, however, has a rarely enforced policy in place that forbids sexual or romantic relationships between current students and employees. Thunder River is a very small community, and residents of the town often take courses at the college as a part of its non-degree community education and job training programs. This makes it impractical to be strict about forbidding all student/employee relationships.

Dr. Lukas is bound by therapeutic confidentiality requirements to keep Michaela's situation to himself, but he wonders whether there might be something he ought to do, as an employee at Thunder River Junior College, relative to the violation of college policy.

Exercises

1. Identify the central ethical problem and then briefly describe the ethically relevant details of this case.

2. For each of the normative theories you've studied so far, briefly describe how the theory might address the problem and details you describe in (1). Your goal in this task is to pick out a claim that you can treat as the conclusion of an ethical argument either for or against reporting Michaela's boyfriend to the Human Resources manager at the college.

3. Come up with two arguments – one *for* turning him in and one *against* – using any of the normative theories you've studied so far. Present each argument as a list of ordered premises leading to a conclusion (use the simple model on p. 6 for guidance).

4. Come up with at least one good objection to each of your proposed arguments. Explain why you think it is a good objection.

5. Respond to the objections – that is, imagine how you might defend each argument by changing a premise, undermining the premises of the objection, etc.

6. Discussion questions: What difference (if any) would the following hypothetical changes in circumstance make to your judgment about whether or not Dr. Lukas should report Michaela's boyfriend to HR? Explain.
   a. Dr. Lukas is also counseling the faculty member who is dating Michaela.
   b. While Michaela took a class with her faculty boyfriend before their relationship began, she is currently not in any classes with him.
   c. Michaela and the professor started dating during a period when she wasn't enrolled at the college, and are currently engaged to be married.

RESOURCES AND INDEX

ONLINE RESOURCES AND FURTHER READING

A small collection of resources for students, including cases, journals discussing the latest research, and a few source texts for ethical theory and application.

Online Resources

The Stanford Encyclopedia of Philosophy:
http://www.ethicsweb.ca/resources/

The Association for Practical and Professional Ethics:
http://appe.indiana.edu/

The Journal of Practical Ethics:
http://www.jpe.ox.ac.uk/

The Society for Ethics Across the Curriculum:
http://www.rit.edu/~w-ethics/seac/

The Hale Chair in Applied Ethics (Rochester Institute of Technology):
http://www.rit.edu/~w-ethics/

The Markkula Center for Applied Ethics (Santa Clara University)
http://www.scu.edu/ethics/

The Robert J. Kutak Center for the Teaching and Study of Applied Ethics at the University of Nebraska (Lincoln):
http://ethics.unl.edu/

The Center for Practical Bioethics
https://www.practicalbioethics.org/

Further Reading

Beauchamp, Tom L. *Case Studies in Business, Ethics, and Society.* 5th ed. New York: Pearson Education Inc. 2004.

Frey, R. G. and Christopher Welman, editors. *A Companion to Applied Ethics (Blackwell Companions to Philosophy).* London: Wiley-Blackwell. 2003.

Singer, Peter. *Applied Ethics (Oxford Readings in Philosophy).* New York: Oxford University Press, USA. 1986.

LaFolette, Hugh and Ingmar Persson, editors. *The Blackwell Guide to Ethical Theory (Blackwell Philosophy Guides).*

Theory and Practice

INDEX

ABOUT THE AUTHOR

L. M. Bernhardt is currently an independent scholar. She did her undergraduate work at Knox College in Galesburg, IL and received her MA and PhD in philosophy from the University of Illinois (Urbana-Champaign), where she completed a dissertation on Kant's ethics. Her other philosophical interests include the philosophy and ethics of information, aesthetics (the philosophy of music and philosophical approaches to popular culture), 18th Century European philosophy, and feminist theory. After a respectable career teaching philosophy to undergraduates at Buena Vista University from 2002-2017, she moved on to new horizons, earning her Masters in Library and Information Science from San José State University in 2016.

Printed in the USA
CPSIA information can be obtained
at www.ICGtesting.com
LVHW010109291223
767658LV00006B/477

Publisher's Note

This publication is designed to provide insightful information in regard to the subject matter covered. It is sold with the understanding that neither the publisher nor the author is engaged in rendering psychological, medical, or other professional services. If expert assistance or counseling is needed, the services of a competent professional should be sought.

While many experiences related in this book are true, names and identifying details have been changed to protect the privacy of the individuals.

***

Copyright © 2017 Michael S. Sorensen

All rights reserved. No part of this publication may be reproduced, distributed, or transmitted in any form or by any means, including photocopying, recording, or other electronic or mechanical methods, without the prior written permission of the publisher, except in the case of brief quotations embodied in critical reviews and certain other noncommercial uses permitted by copyright law. For permission requests, please contact to the publisher at the email address below.

Autumn Creek Press

inquiries@autumncreekpress.com

ISBN-13: 978-0-9991040-0-2

First Edition